Just some of the delights of Tuscany

1. **The hills of Chianti**
   Drive or cycle through forests, vineyards and olive groves (see p113)
2. **The historic centre of San Gimignano**
   The Manhattan of medieval Tuscany, San Gimignano's stone towers dominate the skyline (see p105)
3. **Renaissance Florence**
   Take in the city's artistic wonders and stop for a glass in a lively neighbourhood wine bar (see p98)
4. **Untouched Maremma**
   Explore the natural beauty of Tuscany's Tyrrhenian coast (see p123)
5. **Life is beautiful in Arezzo**
   Visit the excellent trattorias of Arezzo, the backdrop to Roberto Benigni's 1997 film (see p116)
6. **Hilltop Montepulciano**
   Wander ancient alleyways and sample the local Vino Nobile or Vin Santo (see p108)
7. **The Viale dei Cipressi**
   Walk the ancient cypress-lined road to the village of Bolgheri (see p110)
8. **Medieval Siena**
   Take an aperitivo under the Torre del Mangia in Siena's fan-shaped piazza (see p100)

All prices are correct at time of going to press, but are subject to change.

Published 2025 by Académie du Vin Library Ltd
academieduvinlibrary.com
Founders: Steven Spurrier and Simon McMurtrie

Publisher: Hermione Ireland
Series editor: Adam Lechmere
Copy editor: Margaret Watmough
Picture researcher: Silvia Lazzari
Design: Dan Prescott, Imago Create
Maps supplied by Cosmographics
Index: Helen Peters
Proofreader: Jenny Sykes
ISBN: 978-1-917084-61-1
Printed and bound in the EU

Tuscany

Paul Caputo

THE SMART TRAVELLER'S WINE GUIDE

Contents

see p56

see p90

see p111

see p167

Dawn breaks over Antinori's vines on Le Mortelle hill, Lower Maremma

Borgo San Felice, Chianti Classico

Foreword

All great wine regions are unique, but Tuscany – you could say – stands alone. Nowhere else in the wine world has such a history, or such an extraordinary wealth of culture. Here you can find medieval villages, world-famous art collections and hills shaped by vineyards; here wine becomes an authentic expression of the land, born of tradition, passion and innovation.

The enduring appeal of Tuscany is that it can be all things to everyone. Whether you want to spend your days lounging on a sun-warmed terrace sipping a dew-cold Vernaccia, exploring the steep streets of Bolgheri, wandering around Montalcino or visiting five wineries a day (including lunch), then there is something here for you.

We believe that wine is one of the truest ways to tell the story of our region and to welcome those who come here to explore. Wine is a bridge between past and present, between culture and nature, offering a way to experience the soul of Tuscany.

San Felice, nestled in the timeless landscapes of Chianti Classico, embodies this Tuscan authenticity. Surrounded by forests and vineyards, it's a place to rediscover a deep connection with nature.

We hope that every traveller – passionate wine lover, someone discovering wine for the first time or the simply curious – will carry this guide as a trusted companion. Let yourself be inspired by the beauty of Tuscany and captivated by the richness of its wines.

San Felice
Toscana
AD 714

TUSCANY
LIGURIA
COLLI DI LUNI
La Spezia
CANDIA DEI COLLI APUANI
A15
A12
A11
1
Ligurian Sea
COLLINE LUCCHESI
Lucca
MONTECARL
Pisa
River Arn
Livorno
CHIAN COLLI PISAN
LIVORNO
MONTESCUD
TERRATICO DI BIBBONA
Bolgheri
BOLGHE
VAL DI CORNIA
Piombino
ELBA
Isola d'Elba
Florence
Bastia
Corsica
Tyrrhenian Sea
0
20 miles
0
20 kilometres
N
BOLGHERI Wine region
Major town/city
Other town
Railway station
River
Motorway
Main road/Minor road
Railway
Regional boundary
National boundary

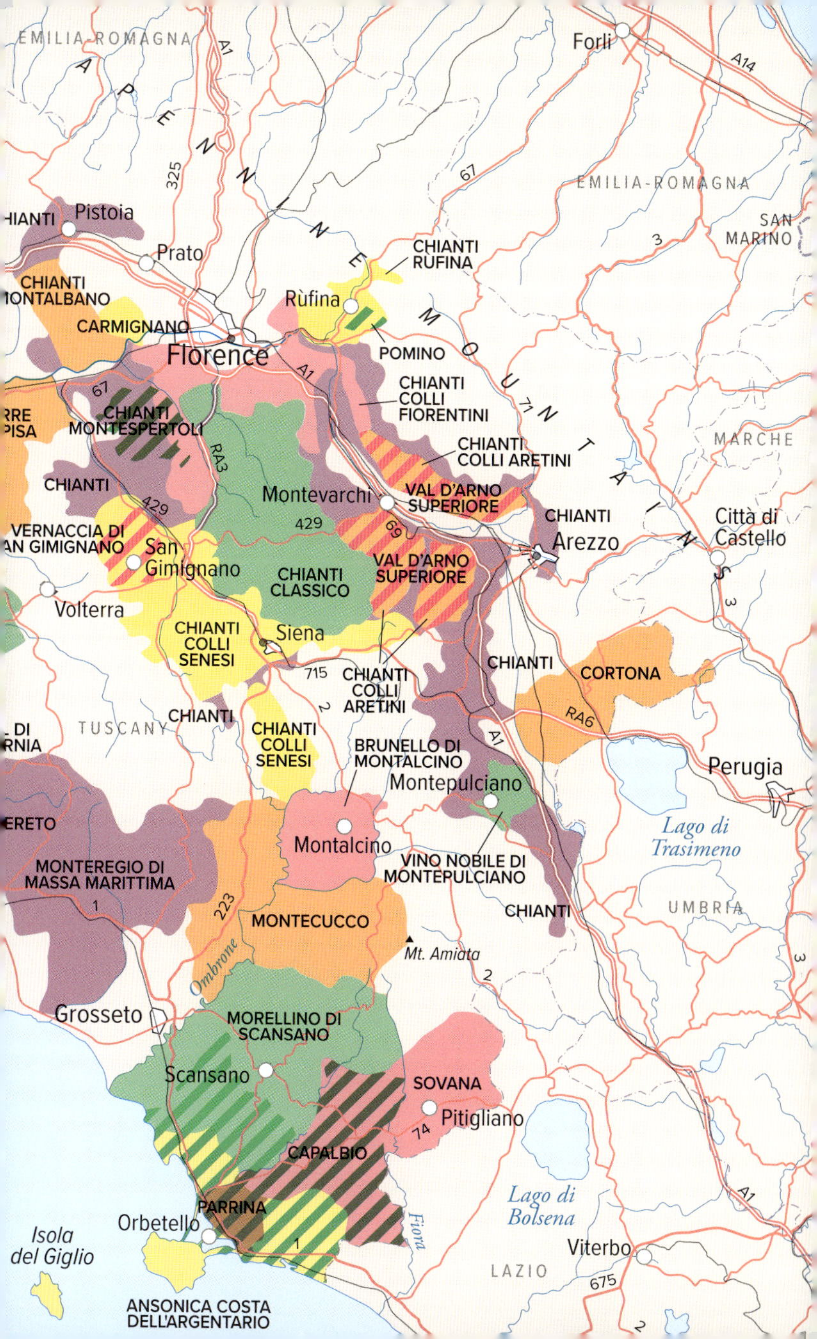

EMILIA-ROMAGNA
APENNINE MOUNTAINS
Forlì
A14
A1
325
67
EMILIA-ROMAGNA
SAN MARINO
3
Pistoia
Prato
CHIANTI RUFINA
CHIANTI MONTALBANO
Rùfina
CARMIGNANO
Florence
POMINO
CHIANTI COLLI FIORENTINI
71
67
CHIANTI MONTESPERTOLI
RA3
CHIANTI COLLI ARETINI
MARCHE
CHIANTI
429
Montevarchi
VAL D'ARNO SUPERIORE
VERNACCIA DI SAN GIMIGNANO
San Gimignano
429
69
CHIANTI
Arezzo
Città di Castello
Volterra
CHIANTI CLASSICO
VAL D'ARNO SUPERIORE
CHIANTI COLLI SENESI
Siena
715
CHIANTI COLLI ARETINI
CHIANTI
CORTONA
TUSCANY
CHIANTI
2
CHIANTI COLLI SENESI
RA6
A1
BRUNELLO DI MONTALCINO
Montepulciano
Perugia
Lago di Trasimeno
Montalcino
VINO NOBILE DI MONTEPULCIANO
MONTEREGIO DI MASSA MARITTIMA
1
223
MONTECUCCO
CHIANTI
UMBRIA
Mt. Amiata
Ombrone
2
Grosseto
MORELLINO DI SCANSANO
Scansano
SOVANA
Pitigliano
74
CAPALBIO
Lago di Bolsena
A1
PARRINA
Orbetello
Isola del Giglio
Fiora
1
Viterbo
LAZIO
675
ANSONICA COSTA DELL'ARGENTARIO
2

Vineyards with San Gimignano on the horizon

Introduction

Everyone knows the *Mona Lisa*, but not everyone notices the landscape behind her. Those hazy hills, winding roads and distant bridges are thought to be inspired by Tuscany. And like *La Gioconda*'s smile, Tuscany's vineyards, olive groves and cypress-lined roads are so familiar that we think we must know them already. But do we?

Nowhere weaves food, wine, landscape and history together quite like Tuscany. For centuries, travellers have come in search of the good life – some drawn to the artistic grandeur of Florence and Siena, others to the quiet beauty of the countryside. Tourism has long been part of daily life here, yet beyond the busiest towns, much of Tuscany remains as it's always been.

This book is for those who think they know Tuscany, and for those who have yet to experience its delights. I've spent over 20 years travelling the region, walking the vineyards, tasting the wines and talking to the people who make them. Each visit reveals something new: not just in the wines, but in the way traditions endure.

Tuscany's towns may be home to Renaissance masterpieces, but they are far more than open-air museums. Wine bars buzz and markets bustle, and just beyond the city walls, the vineyards begin. Food is at the heart of it all. Pecorino from Pienza, bold, peppery olive oil, saffron from San Gimignano. Cinta Senese pigs, raised in oak forests, produce richly flavoured salumi; Chianina cattle for the thick-cut bistecca alla fiorentina; chestnuts, once a rural staple, are still baked into breads and sweets. Every town, every valley, has something its own.

Parts of Tuscany are celebrated worldwide, others remain quietly intriguing; but if you're willing to look beyond the obvious, from wine routes through Bolgheri to how to find the best aperitivo in Florence, here you'll find everything you need to know about the most beguiling wine region in the world.

Paul Caputo
March 2025

History

Tuscany in the Ancient World

We can date winemaking activity in Tuscany back to the Etruscans, who were present from at least the 8th century BCE and probably earlier. Archeological evidence, including wine amphorae and grape seeds, suggests this rather mysterious civilization utilized the region's fertile soils and temperate climate to cultivate the vine. Supported by an early mining industry and extensive maritime expertise, the Etruscans established trading networks across the Mediterranean.

A Roman Feast by Roberto Bompiani, late 19th century

Through these connections, they exchanged knowledge of viticulture and winemaking, particularly with the Greeks, practices they no doubt embraced in their own production.

The Etruscans not only consumed wine locally but also exported it, particularly to Gaul and the Iberian Peninsula. By the 5th century BCE merchant ships loaded with goods frequently skirted the ancient French coastline. One wrecked ship was found to be carrying 4,000 terracotta amphorae, the equivalent of about 40,000 litres of wine. The Celts to the north were also thirsty customers. This trade surely contributed significantly to the region's economy, establishing its reputation for wine production centuries before the Roman Empire.

When Rome's armies eventually conquered in the 3rd century BCE, the victors inherited the region's vineyards and, more importantly, knowledge. Under Roman administration, Tuscany became an important centre for viticulture, with expanded vineyard planting and improved winemaking technologies. Roman innovations included the use of wooden barrels for storage and clay amphorae for transportation, enabling wider distribution of Tuscan wines throughout the empire.

'The Greek poets had already admired Etruria's sweet nectar'

Of course, in those days, wine wasn't quite as we know it today. Bad grapes and unskilled winemaking were often mitigated by infusing herbs, spices and honey for a sweeter taste. Preserving wine was the fundamental challenge, meaning that bacterial spoilage was frequent, and tolerated insofar as it could be disguised.

Nevertheless, Tuscany's geographic diversity still shaped its early wines. The region's rolling hills, characterized by clay, limestone and sand, and in parts by volcanic tuff, allowed for production of wines with distinct identity. The Greek poets had already admired

Etruria's sweet nectar; early Roman agricultural texts, such as those by Columella and Pliny the Elder, continued the praise, commenting on the appeal of certain varieties and highlighting their importance in the broader Roman wine market.

Despite their achievements, Roman winemaking practices often prioritized quantity over quality to meet the empire's vast demand. Yield was high, and wine was often cut with water, partly to weaken it, but also to make it go further. Culturally, however, wine was extremely important: Bacchus, god of wine and festivity, generally brought his lustful satyrs and dancing nymphs to the party and heartily encouraged its consumption.

The Middle Ages: monasteries and city states

The collapse of the Western Roman Empire in the 5th century CE marked a period of upheaval across Europe, including Tuscany. Vineyards suffered neglect as political and social structures disintegrated. Winemaking, and more

The Abbey of Sant'Antimo, Montalcino

importantly, the commitment to work the vineyards on any meaningful scale, survived largely due to the efforts of the Catholic Church. Monasteries and abbeys, particularly those affiliated with the Benedictines, became vital to the preservation of viticultural knowledge and traditions.

Monastic communities in Tuscany, such as the Abbey of Sant'Antimo, maintained vines as part of their agricultural activities, but the resulting wine was essential for religious ceremonies and this provided a strong incentive to continue cultivation, even in uncertain times. Monks also documented their practices – the basis for future refinement. Their dedication ensured that viticulture remained a constant presence in Tuscany.

By the 10th century, feudalism began to stabilize the region. Landowners, including the church and noble families, recognized the economic potential of vineyards. Grapes became a valuable commodity, often used as a form of payment or tribute. The establishment of medieval trade routes further boosted wine commerce, with Tuscan wines finding markets in the northern city states of Venice, Milan and Genoa. The port of Pisa facilitated links with England, France and Spain.

Viticulture in the later Middle Ages also saw a shift in focus towards specific terroirs. Certain areas became associated with higher-quality wines. Records from the period reference the prominence of vineyards in Chianti and other now-famous regions such as Montepulciano, while trade guilds sought to protect and promote their respective interests.

Medieval Tuscany was dominated by the rise of powerful city states and their ruling families, many of whom invested in vineyards as both a commercial trading opportunity and a symbol of wealth. Such competition fuelled tension and conflict, most notably between Florence and Siena. Territory shifted back and forth through the rivalry and political intrigue, but legend has it that a more definitive outcome in the balance of power was settled, essentially, by a black rooster – a symbol you'll see entwined with the story

The story of the Black Rooster

The black rooster is everywhere in Tuscany: on restaurant windows, on the sides of buildings, as souvenir fridge magnets and key rings and, most importantly, on the necks of Chianti Classico wine bottles. More than just a trademark, it represents centuries of history and the territorial rivalry between Florence and Siena. During the Middle Ages, the two city-states frequently clashed over control of Chianti, then the most important winemaking region. To settle the dispute, a race was proposed. Each city would send a

knight at sunrise, departing when their rooster crowed, and where they met would mark the boundary. The Florentines, choosing a black rooster, kept it hungry so that it crowed early, well before dawn. The Sienese, opting for a well-fed white rooster, waited for the natural morning light. As a result, the Florentine knight gained a significant advantage, meeting his Sienese rival just 12km north of Siena at Fonterutoli. Florence secured control over most of Chianti, shaping its future. Art lovers may notice the allegorical presence of the rooster, symbol of the Lega del Chianti, in a ceiling panel painted by Giorgio Vasari in 1565, in the Palazzo Vecchio, Florence.

of Chianti Classico (see p18). It is during this period however that many of Tuscany's famous wine properties find their roots.

The Renaissance: the great families

As the medieval period gave way to the Renaissance, which spanned roughly from the 14th to the 17th century, Tuscany advanced economically, culturally and artistically. During this transformative period, viticulture also evolved from a largely subsistence-based activity into a more commercially significant enterprise. The same old challenges were inherited, of course; inclement weather and rudimentary farming techniques often led to inconsistent yields and quality. Nevertheless, the perseverance of the church and the feudal system ensured a degree of continuity and ultimately set the foundations for a great revival.

The ongoing development of Florence, Siena and Pisa brought wealth and a growing appreciation for fine goods, including wine. Smaller towns such as Lucca, Volterra, San Gimignano, Montepulciano and Arezzo were also in the ascendancy. Prominent families played a pivotal role in elevating wine's status, making it an essential part of banquets, diplomacy and artistic expression. Tuscan wine became a symbol of prestige, embedded in the region's politics and culture. Ensuring that good wine ran freely at the table was enshrined in aristocratic etiquette. Has anything changed?

'White wine made from Vernaccia was first mentioned in 1276'

The Medici family, who dominated much of Tuscany's political and cultural life, left a lasting impact on its viticulture. Their vast estates fostered agricultural innovation, while their patronage of the arts, particularly painting, often resulted in lofty depictions of wine. The

Renaissance reimbued wine with its classical connotations of abundance, Bacchanalian pleasures, and humanity's timeless connections to the land, quite apart from

its prominent Christian symbolism. Across multiple generations, the Medicis' long-standing commitment to Renaissance ideals established an ethos that holds true to this day. Famous wine families, such as the Frescobaldis and Antinoris, pioneers of the Super-Tuscans (see p35), continue to embody those ideals today by linking a similar reverence for heritage and artistic expression.

Often a pawn of statecraft, the period also marked a growing use of regulatory instruments to control wine production and trade. White wine made from Vernaccia, for instance, was first mentioned in a tax document in 1276, indicating the commune of San Gimignano's efforts to manage the import and export of wine. In 1385, Giovanni di Piero Antinori joined the Florentine Winemakers' Guild with the intention of overseeing trade in the city, marking the Antinori family's entry into a wine tradition that endures today. Similarly, the establishment of the *Lega del Chianti* (Chianti League) in the late 14th century as a military and administrative organization under Florentine control emphasized the region's economic value. The league

The barrel cellar at Antinori, Chianti Classico

governed key villages, such as Radda, Gaiole, Castellina and later Greve, which formed the early heart of the Chianti wine region. The organization took the symbol of the black rooster.

Early notions of branding took root during this period. A number of noble families personalized wine with their insignia and no doubt lobbied to protect their interests. For example, harvest dates were eventually governed, reflecting concerns over quality. Unscrupulous farmers and merchants sometimes picked early to gain a competitive edge, but released bitter, underripe wines in the process. With long-term preservation still a challenge, most wine was consumed young and well before the hot summer months finished off remaining supplies. There was money to be made satisfying pent-up demand in the weeks preceding the next vintage.

'Chianti, Carmignano and Montepulciano gained reputations for excellence'

This period also saw advances in vineyard management and winemaking techniques. Written records, such as Pietro de' Crescenzi's *Opus Ruralium Commodorum* (The Book of Rural Benefits), provided detailed guidance on vineyard planting, pruning and harvest timing, reflecting an increasing focus on consistency and quality. These advancements, frequently born out of competition, are a reminder of today's challenges, and the unassailable influence of market demands on innovation. If someone is making better wine for a better price, you either improve or fail.

Regional characteristics in wine started to emerge clearly. By the 16th century, Chianti was already recognized for its distinctiveness, with early documentation praising its quality. Other areas, such as Carmignano and

Montepulciano, also gained reputations for excellence, laying the groundwork for Tuscany's modern appellations. By the end of the Renaissance, backed by wealthy patrons,

Tuscan wine had firmly established its identity. The blend of regional pride, improved production practices and a growing international reputation set the stage for Tuscany to emerge as one of the world's most celebrated wine regions in the centuries to come.

The 18th Century: modernization

The 18th century, or the *Settecento*, was characterized by the early stirrings of modernization. Progress was tempered by economic setbacks, but a significant moment occurred in 1716, when Grand Duke Cosimo III de' Medici issued an edict identifying and protecting four key wine-producing areas: Chianti, Carmignano, Pomino and Valdarno di Sopra. This decree was among the first formal attempts at appellation regulation in Europe, demonstrating an early understanding of the importance of terroir, quality control and the politics of territorial brand.

'Agronomists introduced modern techniques for planting, pruning, and harvesting'

Medici influence waned with the death of Gian Gastone de' Medici in 1737, essentially marking the end of the dynasty. Tuscany then came under the rule of the Habsburg-Lorraine family, with Francisco Stefano of Lorraine becoming Grand Duke. Under this leadership, the 1750s saw a series of reforms aimed at revitalizing agriculture. The tenant farming system, known as *mezzadria* ('divides in half'), was restructured to incentivize better land management, indirectly benefiting vineyard practices. Publications by agronomists introduced modern techniques for planting, pruning and harvesting grapes, encouraging landowners to adopt more systematic approaches to winemaking.

These advancements aligned with the broader agricultural reforms initiated by Pietro Leopoldo, who became Grand Duke in 1765. His progressive policies included rational land use and the promotion of trade, which allowed Tuscan wines to reach new markets. The late 18th century saw further recognition for Chianti's status, now well established since the 1716 edict. The famous agronomist Giovanni Cosimo Villifranchi reinforced the nature of Chianti's boundaries and viticulture in his 1773 text *Oenologia Toscana o sia Memoria Sopra i Vini ed in Specie Toscani*. This was another small step in the culture of protected origin wines. By the time Pietro Leopoldo's reign ended in 1790, his reforms had further enriched the Tuscan countryside's reputation as one of the world's great sources of wine.

1800–1945: upheaval and recovery

The 19th century was a time of both upheaval and recovery for Tuscan viticulture. Following the Napoleonic Wars, which interfered with much of Europe's agricultural economy, Tuscany began to rebuild its wine industry. The vine-eating pest phylloxera decimated vineyards towards the end of the 1800s. This infestation, combined with the spread of powdery mildew, led to significant losses, not only in plantings but also in diversity.

Tens of thousands of hectares were grubbed up, and although efforts to combat phylloxera, through the grafting of European vines onto resistant American rootstocks, eventually stabilized the industry, it would take decades for Tuscan viticulture to fully recover. Some might argue that it still hasn't. There are today over 120 different recognized grape varieties in Tuscany, but Sangiovese covers the majority of planted surface area.

By the middle of the 1800s, industrial and political changes were sweeping through the Italian peninsula.

Tuscany experienced the effects of unification in 1861, and once the dust had settled, the *Risorgimento* ('Rising Again') brought new economic opportunities, with an emerging middle class that began to consume and demand higher-quality wines. This shift in consumer expectation spurred some landowners to experiment with improved viticultural techniques.

Bettino Ricasoli of Castello di Brolio was one such character. Known as the Iron Baron, he published his recipe for Chianti in 1872. Having pulled up many international varieties, such as the high-yielding Gamay, he planted those he considered more local. His observations led him to articulate a vision for Chianti wines. He called for seven parts Sangiovese (for bouquet and quality), two parts Canaiolo Nero (for softness) and one part Malvasia Bianca Lunga (for aroma). Chianti's required composition has changed since then, but crafting a wine's style around the inherent characteristics of individual grapes was very progressive.

The early 20th century brought significant challenges. The First World War disrupted agricultural labour and left the countryside economically strained. Many small farmers abandoned their vineyards, exacerbating a trend towards larger estates and a focus on volume over quality. This decline was mirrored in the *mezzadria* sharecropping

Castello di Brolio in Chianti, owned by the Ricasoli family for 800 years

system, which became increasingly unsustainable as economic pressures mounted and people sought alternative employment in the cities.

The interwar years saw tentative steps towards recovery, particularly in Chianti, where producers began to codify and promote the region's wines. The *Consorzio Vino Chianti* (Chianti Wine Consortium), established in 1924, was one of Italy's earliest attempts to regulate and protect the quality of a specific wine region. Intriguingly, wine was re-positioned as a national beverage under Fascism, and given government support. The economic struggles of the Great Depression in the USA were felt internationally, and then World War II brought further devastation, with vineyards damaged during military campaigns and agricultural labour structures disrupted once again. By 1945, Tuscan winemaking was at a crossroads. A different business model would be needed, and one was duly developed as part of a dramatic revival.

World War II to the present

The cultural shift that followed two devastating world wars was significant. Alongside the practical realities of reduced man-power in rural communities, many smallholders either sold or abandoned their vineyards in a bid to meet basic post-war demands. The *mezzadria* system of tenant farming persisted into the mid century, but in disproportionately favouring the landowner, the system became unsustainable and collapsed. Growing grapes and making wine increasingly required capital, business processes and customers. Fortunately, demand from burgeoning cities boomed, but as is so often the case, when yields increased, quality dropped. Chianti was always popular, but there was growing interest in the region's other red wines. Brunello di Montalcino and Vino Nobile di Montepulciano quickly filled every restaurant cellar.

A turning point came in the 1960s and 1970s, when a new generation of winemakers began to focus on making good wine rather than chasing volume. Much of the innovation

Montalcino

came from long-established, noble families. The Super-Tuscans emerged, led by iconic names such as Sassicaia in 1968 (the first Super-Tuscan to be released) and Tignanello. These wines, made outside the traditional DOC regulations, combined the indigenous Sangiovese with classic French varieties like Cabernet Sauvignon and Merlot. Their success on the global stage challenged the region's regulatory framework and forced a rethinking of what Tuscan wine could, and indeed should, be.

In the late 20th century, Tuscan winemaking benefitted from more advancements in technology and a renewed focus on terroir. Improved vineyard management practices and temperature-controlled fermentation became the norm, while investment in new barrels and maturation space helped small producers craft wines with greater balance, longevity and consistency. With the general state of wine much improved, the collective focus turned to the international marketing of ever-smaller territories. Despite Tuscany's great heritage, much of the tradition wine lovers lean into today was crafted in the last 50 years or so. Italy's DOC system gathered pace in the 1970s and

Brunellogate: the story of a scandal

Between 2008 and 2009, Brunello di Montalcino was rocked by a scandal known as Brunellopoli (or Brunellogate, as some journalists dubbed it). Allegations surfaced that leading producers had blended other grape varieties into their wines. They were looking to create a darker, fruitier and fuller-bodied style to appeal to international markets, especially when difficult, cooler vintages produced a leaner style. Brunello's DOCG regulations stipulate the wines must be 100% Sangiovese; adding any other grape was a violation of the appellation's rules. The consequences were severe. Italian authorities quarantined vineyards and confiscated millions of bottles; US regulators temporarily blocked imports of uncertified Brunello. Though the scandal temporarily tainted the region's reputation, it also triggered a renewed commitment to Sangiovese's purity amongst growers. Producers reaffirmed the DOCG's rules, rejecting proposals to allow other grapes into the wine. It also led to extensive research into Sangiovese's colour stability, anthocyanins and pigment development, and therefore the ability to detect the presence of other varieties in a wine. Today, Brunello has not only regained its standing but has emerged stronger, with a deeper scientific and cultural appreciation for the grape that defines it.

amendments have been made to boundaries, production rules and labelling requirements ever since. In the early 1980s, Brunello di Montalcino became one of the first Italian wines to receive DOCG status. Others followed. New appellations kept coming, each offering, in theory at least, a window into some very specific terroir. Yet, having tied themselves up in rules and regulations, a more flexible Toscana IGP classification was established in 1992 to keep wineries competitive, and this is widely used today. For the purist, there are now a rather intimidating 11 DOCGs, 41 DOCs and 6 IGPs to grapple with.

The first quarter of the 21st century has brought further evolution. Organic and biodynamic practices have gained traction, with producers motivated by varying combinations of integrity, opportunism and the mounting evidence that chemicals degrade vineyard health. Healthy vines provide resistance and adaptability, concepts now being tested by undeniable climatic change. With literally thousands of wineries made up of farmers, families, investors and larger corporates, Tuscany continues to balance tradition with progress, and maintains its status as one of the world's most dynamic and respected wine regions.

Antinori, Chianti Classico

Cement tanks at Tenuta Argentiera, Bolgheri

Geography

Tuscany's undulating landscape, the golden fields rippling in the breeze, cypress-lined roads, stone farmhouses and a medieval town sitting serenely in the background, is often romanticized. Yet beyond the postcard imagery lies a region of remarkable variety, where altitude, climate and proximity to the sea subtly but decisively shape its wines.

Argentiera

To the west, a rugged coastline meets the Tyrrhenian Sea, its sandy shores and fishing villages giving way to vineyards that thrive in the maritime climate. Central Tuscany, often considered the soul of rural Italian life, is a patchwork of rolling hills, olive groves and vineyards, punctuated by ancient towns, that have shaped the region's agricultural traditions for centuries. Further east, the Apennine Mountains form a natural boundary, their wooded foothills offering a different expression of Tuscany – one where the climate is cooler, the terrain more dramatic and the wines influenced by altitude as much as by tradition.

Tuscany's varied topography creates a complex interplay of microclimates and growing conditions, shaping the wines in ways both obvious and imperceptible. Though its landscapes flow seamlessly into one another, broad distinctions emerge between the coastal west, the central heartland and the high-altitude east. Each of these areas offers conditions that define the style and identity of the wines produced within them.

Western Tuscany

Western Tuscany unfolds along the Tyrrhenian coast, stretching from the historic city of Pisa down past Livorno and Bolgheri to the sun-drenched plains of the Maremma near Grosseto. This is a landscape shaped by its maritime proximity. The sea is a constant presence along the *Costa degli Etruschi*, moderating temperatures, influencing wind patterns and defining the character of the wines grown here.

The climate along the coast is warmer and more stable than in central Tuscany. Milder winters allow for early budbreak, while steady breezes keep excessive humidity in check, reducing disease pressure in the vineyards. The growing season is long, with abundant sunshine ensuring full ripeness in the grapes. The difference between day and night temperatures is less extreme than in the inland hills, leading often to wines that are richer, softer and more fruit-forward, but with a freshness that is a defining feature of the coastal air.

WESTERN TUSCANY

Geologically, western Tuscany is diverse, but it lacks the compact limestone and schist formations found further inland. Much of the area is composed of alluvial soils, clay, sand and pockets of marine deposits, remnants of an ancient seabed. These elements contribute to well-draining soils that suit Bordeaux varieties particularly well. In Bolgheri, the mix of gravel and sand creates structured yet refined wines, and it is one of the reasons why Cabernet Sauvignon and Merlot thrive here. The Super-Tuscan movement, which first gained international recognition in the 1970s, owes much to this coastal environment, where Bordeaux grapes ripen fully but retain elegance and balance.

Further south, in the Maremma, the land flattens, and the climate grows hotter, particularly inland beyond the influence of the sea. Vineyards here can produce powerful, fruit-forward wines, yet those planted closer to the coast benefit from cooling breezes, allowing for a broader range of styles and more aromatic complexity. While Sangiovese remains important, there is also a growing presence of Syrah, Vermentino and even native varieties like Ciliegiolo.

Further north, Pisa and its surroundings, despite being better known for their history than their vineyards, also play a role in Tuscany's coastal viticulture. The hills beyond the city offer favourable conditions for both red and white wines, with coastal winds helping to preserve acidity, particularly in white grapes. The wines from this area, which are little known outside Tuscany, tend to be soft and fruity, with maritime freshness.

Central Tuscany

Central Tuscany is the region's viticultural core, a landscape of gentle hills, forested ridges and medieval towns that have been intertwined with wine for centuries. Stretching from the vineyards surrounding San Gimignano in the northwest through Chianti Classico, and further south to Montalcino and Montepulciano, this is where Tuscany's most iconic wines take shape.

The climate here is more variable than on the coast, with greater swings between daytime heat and cooler nights. This diurnal range is particularly important for Sangiovese, Tuscany's dominant red grape, as it helps to preserve acidity and structure while allowing for full ripening. Rainfall is more evenly spread throughout the year, though certain areas – such as the southern slopes of Montalcino – receive

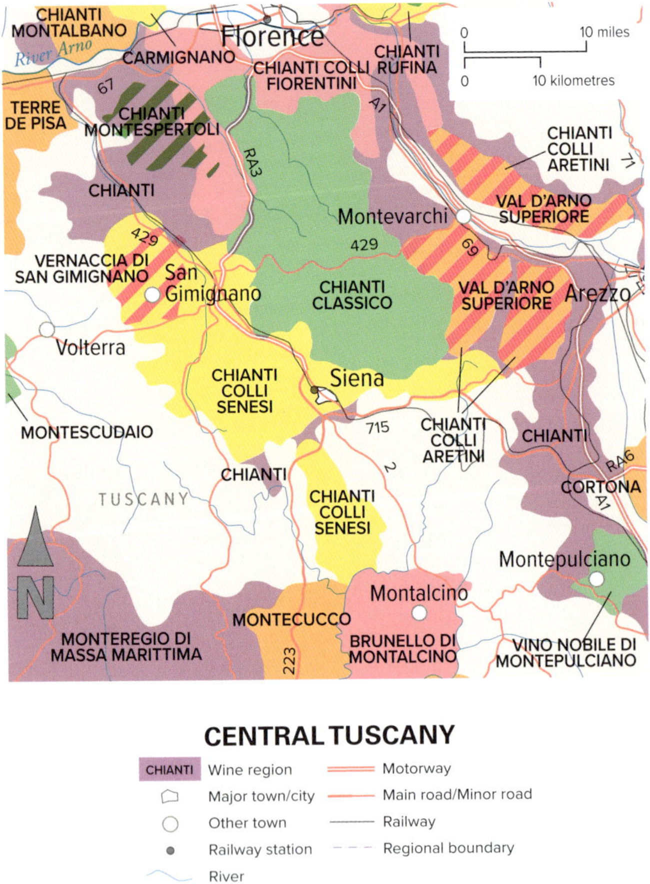

CENTRAL TUSCANY

less rain, leading to warmer, drier conditions that influence the power and depth of the wines.

Elevation is another defining feature. Vineyards in Chianti Classico, between 250 and 600 metres, produce Sangiovese with brighter acidity, more red fruit character and a more linear structure. The best sites benefit from a balance of warmth and ventilation, avoiding excessive

Super-Tuscans

In the late 1940s, when the Marchese Mario Incisa della Rocchetta, owner of Tenuta San Guido in Bolgheri, bottled a few hundred litres of Cabernet Sauvignon and Cabernet Franc for his family and friends, he might not have guessed it would become one of Italy's – the world's – most famous wines.

Sassicaia was released commercially in 1971, when the 1968 vintage was put on the market. It started a small revolution. The Super Tuscan movement's impetus was a response to rigid DOC regulations, which dictated which grape varieties must be used – for example Sangiovese in Chianti – leaving little room for experimentation. Tuscany's historic winemaking families felt these rules stifled their ability to create wines that could compete with the great reds of Bordeaux.

Sassicaia was the first major departure from tradition. Made primarily from Cabernet Sauvignon, it was unlike anything else produced in Tuscany at the time and laid the foundations for Bolgheri to emerge as a world-class wine region. A few years later in 1974, Antinori introduced the 1971 Tignanello, which reduced the proportion of Sangiovese and incorporated Cabernet Sauvignon. The fact that it was produced within Chianti Classico marked another significant break from convention. This was followed in the 1980s by the Cabernet-Merlot dominant Ornellaia, and later Masseto, a 100 per cent Merlot, both of which reinforced Bolgheri's reputation as Italy's answer to Bordeaux.

Initially labelled as Vino da Tavola, these wines quickly gained international acclaim, forcing regulatory change and leading to the creation of the Toscana IGP category – and in 1994 the Bolgheri Sassicaia DOC, Tuscany's only single-producer appellation.

Today, nearly every Tuscan estate bottles a premium Toscana IGP wine, making the term Super Tuscan less of a rebellion and more a badge of quality. The movement has lost some of its disruptive edge, ironically creating plenty of new production regulations in Bolgheri DOC, but remains a huge part of the identity of Tuscan wine.

ripeness while ensuring complexity. In contrast, the lower-altitude vineyards of Montalcino experience a warmer and drier climate, resulting in Brunello wines that are deeper, darker and more concentrated.

‘Tuscany’s history of winemaking is as important as its geography’

Soil diversity plays a role, though it is not the singular defining factor. San Gimignano, known for its white Vernaccia, sits on sandy and clay-rich soils, contributing to wines with freshness and a mineral edge. Montepulciano, home to Vino Nobile di Montepulciano, has a mix of clay, silt and limestone, producing Sangiovese-based wines that tend to be fuller and plusher than Chianti, but don’t match the body and power of Brunello di Montalcino.

The history of winemaking in this part of Tuscany is as important as its geography. The vineyards of Chianti Classico, Montalcino and Montepulciano are not just defined by their altitude or soil, but by centuries of tradition, cultural refinement and evolving philosophies of viticulture. Here, the balance between heritage and modernity, structure and elegance, warmth and freshness, defines the wines in ways that geography alone cannot.

Eastern Tuscany

Eastern Tuscany, stretching towards the Apennine foothills, is a quieter, less familiar side of the region’s viticulture. It lacks the international recognition of Chianti Classico or Montalcino, yet the vineyards around Arezzo, Valdarno di Sopra and Cortona are increasingly proving that wines of finesse and balance can be made here. Indeed, they were in the past – why shouldn’t they find their place with contemporary drinkers?

The Apennines act as a natural barrier, influencing the climate in distinct ways. Cooler air descends into the valleys,

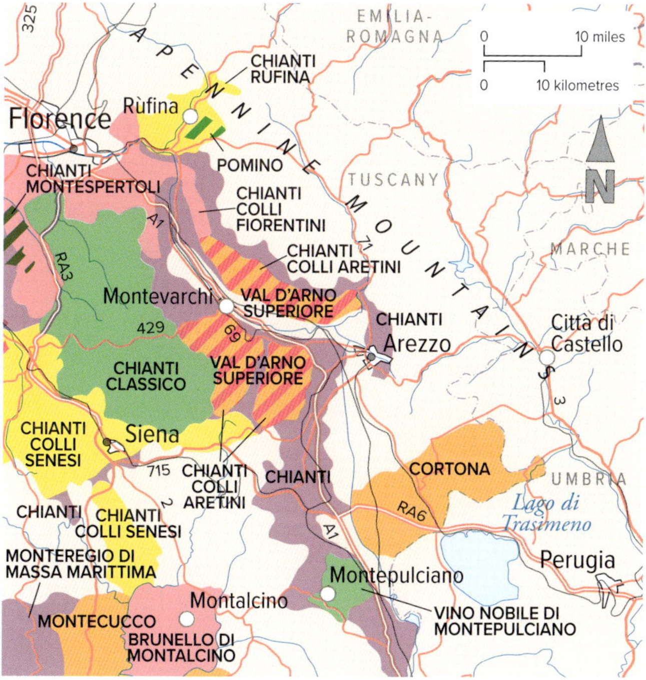

EASTERN TUSCANY

CHIANTI	Wine region		Motorway
	Major town/city		Main road/Minor road
	Other town		Railway
	Railway station		Regional boundary
	River		

moderating summer heat and extending the growing season. This is particularly beneficial for Sangiovese, which here tends to retain higher acidity and more delicate aromatics than in the warmer parts of Tuscany. The greater variation between daytime and nighttime temperatures allows for slower ripening, a key factor in achieving complexity without excessive alcohol.

The Valdarno di Sopra, a historic winemaking area that once supplied the Medici court, benefits from higher elevations and well-ventilated vineyards. While Sangiovese remains the backbone of winemaking here, there is also a growing interest in Cabernet Sauvignon and Merlot, continuing the legacy of Bordeaux varieties in Tuscany. These wines tend to show refinement rather than power, shaped as much by the altitude as by the region's deep viticultural history.

'Cortona's elegant wines are often closer in style to the northern Rhône than to the Tuscan coast'

Further east, Cortona has emerged as a small, but exciting region for Syrah. The area's combination of warm days, cool nights and well-draining soils provides near-ideal conditions for the variety. The resulting wines are elegant and structured, often showcasing peppery spice and dark fruit, closer in style to the northern Rhône than to Tuscany's coastal expressions.

In Arezzo and the surrounding valleys, white wines have also gained recognition, particularly Trebbiano Toscana and Chardonnay, benefitting from the region's natural freshness and elevated sites. While historically overlooked, eastern Tuscany is quietly redefining itself, producing wines that reflect both the influence of altitude and the enduring traditions of Tuscan viticulture.

Fattoria Fibbiano, Terricciola, Pisa

Dry stone wall terraces at Tenuta Sette Cieli, Bolgheri

The grapes

Sangiovese, which accounts for around 85% of Tuscany's vineyards, dominates the viticultural activity of the region and is responsible for many different styles of wine. Its various biotypes and clones can give very different personalities and provide the backbone for important appellations such as the two Chiantis, Brunello di Montalcino, Vino Nobile di Montepulciano, Morellino di Scansano and Carmignano.

The many faces of Sangiovese entrench the concept of terroir and remind us of the purpose and value of appellations. Officially, however, Tuscany has more than 100 registered grape varieties. Many are very old, indigenous and extremely rare. Hundreds of small wineries work each year to maintain this vinous heritage, and, for the curious wine lover, there is a great deal of diversity to ponder. Most of them play a supporting role, but a few – Ciliegiolo, for example – make interesting single varietal wines. International varieties of course have had a huge effect on Tuscany's reputation, in the form of Super-Tuscans like Sassicaia (see p35). White grapes are enjoying a renaissance of sorts too. Vermentino in particular is becoming very popular, while the often unappreciated Vernaccia and Trebbiano Toscano are being cultivated by producers dedicated to finding their finest Tuscan expression.

The reds

Sangiovese

Sangiovese is by far the most important grape variety in Tuscany – some might say in all of Italy. At its best it produces structured and elegant wines capable of ageing and improving for many years. Over time, Sangiovese has developed a subtly different character to adapt to different environments. These mutations are distinct biotypes – natural variations, rather than clones. In Tuscany there are three biotype names that really matter: Brunello in Montalcino, Prugnolo Gentile in Montepulciano and Morellino, found in Scansano. In one style or another, you're going to see Sangiovese everywhere you go. Why, you may ask, does this grape take on so many different names in such a small area? How different are these wines?

In Montalcino, the wines are considerably more robust than elsewhere. Brunello has small berries and thick skins, resulting in a tannic wine that needs time to mature and soften. Patience is rewarded, though. After time in oak, the wines develop aromas of dark cherry, leather and spice. The

best will be good for 30 years. Maybe more. Sangiovese is integral to Montalcino's contemporary identity and is the only territory that enforces its use *in purezza* (Brunello di Montalcino DOCG is the only Sangiovese appellation in Tuscany that requires Sangiovese to be 100% of the blend). So important is the idea of what Montalcino's flagship DOCG wine should be, a national scandal erupted in 2008 when some producers were found to have slipped in other varieties. The controversy resulted in legal action and convictions. The use of other grapes is not only illegal, to do so is considered sacrilege (see p27).

Sangiovese is also an excellent conduit of terroir in the Chianti Classico villages. The area's famous *galestro* (flaky grey schist) soils give Sangiovese a lighter, more floral expression. In Greve-in-Chianti, the soils are richer in clay and limestone, producing a floral but plump version of Sangiovese. On the higher, colder slopes of Radda-in-

Chianti, it can be particularly racy. The nuances are endless. Further north, the high, weather-beaten Rufina territory, closer to Florence, Sangiovese is lighter and fresher again.

Sangiovese and its clones and biotypes have developed over centuries; its many different names, derived from local dialects, complicate the situation still further. We're learning more about this important grape all the time, through genetic studies and other research. What we know for certain is that at its best, Sangiovese produces wines of wonderful complexity, big and bold, laden with fruit and brisk acidity, and capable of decades of ageing.

As the primary protagonist in Chianti Classico, Brunello di Montalcino and Vino Nobile di Montepulciano, as well as a host of up-and-coming territories such as Scansano, Maremma, Montecucco and Carmignano, it is undoubtedly a variety that expresses its surroundings. Precisely what comes from the grape and what comes from the land is still very much part of the magic. The best Sangiovese wines have aromas of fresh cherry, forest fruits, earth, moss and mushroom. Over time they become even more elegant and ethereal.

Ciliegiolo

References to the cultivation of Ciliegiolo in Italy date back to the 1600s. Some believe it has been grown in Tuscany since the Etruscan era. Traditionally a minor blending grape, it was used to soften Sangiovese's tannins and add bright fruit. In the Maremma, particularly in Grosseto, it is now being explored as a single-varietal wine, valued for its freshness and vibrancy.

Ciliegiolo is thought to be a parent of Sangiovese, though conflicting studies make it unclear which came first. Its name derives from *ciliegia* (cherry), a nod to its pronounced red cherry aromas. Its wines are juicy in youth, with herbal undertones that enhance their food-friendly appeal.

Of the 550 hectares planted in Tuscany, around 310 are in the Maremma, where the Mediterranean climate, sunny days

and coastal breezes enhance its fragrance while preserving acidity. Soil plays a key role in shaping its character, with sandy and volcanic terrain lending an energetic profile. Winemakers are experimenting with different techniques to highlight its purity, but its thin skin makes it susceptible to disease, requiring meticulous care.

Once dismissed for its light colour and soft structure, Ciliegiolo is now valued for its easy-drinking charm, particularly for lunchtime wines. Alongside Vermentino, it is becoming a key marker of Maremma's viticultural identity, reflecting the rising interest in indigenous grapes and fresher, lighter styles.

Other local red grapes: Colorino, Canaiolo and Mammolo

There are a lot of minor grape varieties used in Tuscany, most of which support Sangiovese. For centuries they have been the unsung heroes of winemaking. Never quite strong enough to produce a good wine alone, they've contributed their individual personality and given wines a flourish. You'll see them referenced on back labels, particularly in Chianti DOCG wines and in Vino Nobile di Montepulciano DOCG.

Two will be spotted frequently – Colorino and Canaiolo. Colorino is a thick-skinned red grape variety appreciated primarily for its ability to give colour pigment to wines. It was incorporated into Chianti to add a darker hue, an age-old response to Sangiovese's low colour pigment. As with everything in Italian wine, there is complexity below the surface. There are multiple Colorino grapes – Colorino di Valdarno, Colorino di Lucca, Colorino di Pisa – which have subtly different profiles, but when used in small percentages these differences are negligible for most drinkers.

Canaiolo, the other important red blending grape, is one of Tuscany's oldest and most versatile. With its delicate floral aromas, soft tannins and bright acidity, it is considered a suitable counterpoint to Sangiovese. (Bettino Ricasoli's 1872 Chianti recipe (see p24) called for 20% Canaiolo.) Although its prominence has diminished over time, particularly in the region's more prestigious wines, Canaiolo remains a common component of more everyday table wines.

Less common is Mammolo. It produces big fat bunches with lots of juice and very intense aromas of violet. It's sometimes used to add a bit more fruit to Sangiovese, but it's seldom considered complex enough to be taken seriously on its own. The best place to look for Mammolo is as a supporting grape in Vino Nobile di Montepulciano, where some producers uphold Tuscan tradition and avoid using Cabernet or Merlot. It's also used in Carmignano, and even found in lesser-known appellations such as Montecucco DOC and Massa Marittima DOC.

International red grapes: Cabernet Sauvignon, Merlot and Syrah

Cabernet Sauvignon, Cabernet Franc and Merlot have played a transformative role in Tuscany, particularly in the establishment of the influential Super-Tuscan wines that emerged in the 1970s. These classic Bordeaux varieties, now very much international, were originally seen as outsiders in a region dominated by Sangiovese. They have since become important components of the region's viticultural identity, however.

Cabernet Sauvignon, with its powerful structure, dark fruit flavours and tannic backbone, has been a success in Tuscany's warm climate. It is particularly well-suited to the coastal areas of Bolgheri, where the maritime influence moderates temperatures and ensures a gradual phenolic ripening. Here, it is often blended with Merlot and Cabernet Franc to create bold, age-worthy wines.

Merlot has gained a solid reputation in Tuscany, producing wines of remarkable depth and elegance. At the top end, iconic wines such as Masseto are now considered the equals of some of the great wines of Bordeaux. While it excels in the coastal terroirs of Bolgheri and Maremma, it also performs exceptionally well in certain pockets of the Chianti hills. These inland vineyards, with cooler nights and clay-rich soils, produce Merlot wines of surprising structure and balance.

Cabernet Franc, often used in smaller proportions, contributes herbal aromatics, finesse and freshness to Tuscan blends, complementing the richness of Cabernet Sauvignon and the suppleness of Merlot. There is a growing appreciation for Cabernet Franc by itself, and we're likely to see more mono-varietal expressions. Look out for Le Macchiole, Tua Rita and Tenuta Sette Cieli. As the climate warms, Cabernet Franc has the advantage of ripening later than Merlot and Cabernet Sauvignon, thus retaining its acidity and bringing a welcome freshness to blends. Investment in these varieties was driven by an appreciation of the great wines of Bordeaux, coupled with a lingering

Merlot

suspicion that Sangiovese could not consistently produce world-class wines. There's some truth in that: its myriad clones and genetic inconsistencies have made it difficult to harness the grape's full potential. Only now, through rigorous study and clonal selection, are we beginning to see Sangiovese's true capacity for greatness, as evidenced by the exceptional wines of Chianti Classico and Brunello di Montalcino.

The Whites

Trebbiano Toscano

Trebbiano Toscano is one of Italy's most widely planted white varieties. High-yielding and neutral in flavour, it has traditionally been used for table wines or blending. Yet, despite its reputation, it remains integral to Tuscany's viticultural identity, forming the backbone of traditional Vin Santo and attracting a small but growing interest in fine dry wines.

Its natural traits make it ideal for mass production. Vigorous and adaptable, it thrives in various soils and climates. Known as Ugni Blanc in France, it is a key component of Cognac due to its acidity and neutrality. However, when vinified alone, these same qualities can make it seem unremarkable, lacking aromatic depth.

Trebbiano Toscano has strengths and weaknesses. Its thick skins and late ripening give it resistance to diseases like botrytis, and it performs well in Tuscany's warm Mediterranean climate. However, it struggles with water stress in dry summers, and unchecked vigour can lead to excessive yields that dilute quality. Winemakers seeking higher expression employ strict pruning and canopy control to concentrate flavours.

Typically, Trebbiano Toscano produces light, crisp wines with notes of green apple, citrus and white flowers. While often consumed young, its acidity allows it to age well, particularly in oxidative styles like Vin Santo. In this traditional Tuscan dessert wine, Trebbiano (alongside Malvasia Bianca Lunga) is partially dried to intensify sugars before ageing in small barrels, yielding complex, nutty wines with caramel and dried fruit notes.

'Crafting high-quality single-varietal wines and blends, winemakers are revealing the untapped potential of Trebbiano Toscano'

Though overshadowed by Vernaccia and Vermentino, Trebbiano Toscano is gaining renewed attention from winemakers crafting high-quality single-varietal wines and blends. Through lower yields and precise winemaking, they are revealing its untapped potential, elevating it beyond its historic role as a blending grape.

Vermentino

It's best known in Sardinia, but Vermentino is one of Tuscany's most important white grapes, particularly in coastal areas like Bolgheri and Maremma. Well-adapted to the region's maritime climate, Vermentino is valued for its natural freshness and aromatic complexity. The wines are typically light to medium-bodied, with vibrant acidity and bright flavours of citrus, green apple and stone fruit, often accompanied by floral and herbal notes such as thyme and sage. Seen internationally as an enjoyable alternative to Sauvignon Blanc, Vermentino is developing a reputation as a stylish aperitif and a good match with seafood and light Mediterranean dishes.

We're likely to see more of it in the future. In the vineyard, Vermentino has several advantages. It is a heat-tolerant variety, performing well in Tuscany's coastal climates, where, despite being tempered by cooling sea breezes, warm days are getting warmer. This balance helps retain acidity while allowing the fruit to ripen evenly, resulting in wines that are fresh yet flavourful. Vermentino is also well-suited to sandy and well-drained soils, common in the Maremma, which enhance its minerality and lend a subtle saline quality to the wines.

Vermentino is not without its challenges, however. The grape's thin skin makes it vulnerable to botrytis and mildew, particularly in humid vintages, requiring vigilant vineyard management. Achieving the right balance in yields is also critical. Overcropping can lead to dilute wines that lack the

Vermentino

grape's characteristic aromatic intensity. Careful pruning and canopy management are essential to ensure optimal sunlight exposure and airflow around the vines.

In recent years, Vermentino's success has spurred interest in the Maremma Toscana DOC, where producers are focusing on making high-quality single-varietal expressions. Many winemakers ferment in stainless steel to preserve the grape's freshness, while others experiment with subtle oak ageing to add texture and complexity. Commercial realities are important too. Vermentino gives producers a little extra variation in their portfolio. It's nice to have something fresh, fruity and relatively inexpensive as well as premium reds.

Vernaccia

Tuscany's oldest white variety has been cultivated around the town of San Gimignano since at least 1276, when it was first documented. Despite this venerable heritage, Vernaccia struggles to impress the modern wine lover. Throughout the 1990s and early 2000s its reputation suffered as high yields diluted its natural characteristics and led to bland and uninspiring wines.

Vernaccia is notoriously thin-skinned, which makes it susceptible to sunburn in Tuscany's intense summer heat. At

Vernaccia

the same time, it struggles in humid vintages, when its thin skins can harbour fungal diseases and rot. Effective canopy management is crucial, ensuring the bunches are protected from excessive sunlight while maintaining enough airflow to prevent disease. Moreover, reducing yields is essential to enhance concentration and bring out the grape's subtle yet distinctive flavours.

'Some argue Vernaccia is best enjoyed young ... others believe it develops complexity with age'

Vernaccia thrives in sand and clay soils, which are abundant around San Gimignano. These soils are ideal for moderating water stress, particularly during the scorching Tuscan summers when rainfall is scarce, and temperatures soar. The sandy components contribute a lively minerality to the wines, elevating the perception of Vernaccia's muted fruit profile, which typically features notes of citrus, white flowers and bitter almond.

In the cellar, Vernaccia presents additional challenges. One of its defining characteristics is a propensity to oxidize quickly, raising debates about the wine's ageing potential. Some argue it's best enjoyed young for its delicate primary fruit and crisp acidity; others believe it can develop complexity with age. Judicious use of oak can add depth and structure, but too much risks overpowering the grape's delicate flavours.

Despite its challenges, Vernaccia di San Gimignano is undergoing a renaissance, as modern producers focus on quality over quantity. By embracing lower yields, sustainable viticulture and careful winemaking, they are unlocking the potential of this historic grape, creating wines that balance subtlety and complexity with a vibrant expression of their unique terroir.

Classifications and how they work

If you find Italian wine overwhelming, don't worry – you're not alone. Navigating your way around more than 2,000 different grape varieties and hundreds of appellations, all with their own production rules, can be a formidable task. That's without mentioning the vast world of bureaucratic terms and individual vineyard references.

Antinori, Chianti Classico

Unlike France's relatively tidy system, Italy's is layered, constantly evolving and, at times, extremely frustrating. Nevertheless, within this complexity lies a structure that protects the identity of Italy's wines, responds to market realities and allows room for innovation. Although Italian labels can sometimes leave experienced wine lovers scratching their heads, the country's wine law is, in essence, designed to ensure quality by preserving a mix of history, geography and stubborn tradition. To make sense of it all, let's start with the basics. In line with the European Union's framework, Italy has four classifications, which in theory indicate the level of quality.

DOC - Denominazione di Origine Controllata

The DOC classification was modelled on France's AOC system. In its simplest form, it protects both producers and consumers by dictating the boundaries of a production zone, while setting out rules regarding permitted grape varieties, yields and ageing requirements. The system, created in 1963 and still in place today, includes over 330 appellations classified as DOC. Some of the best appellations have been promoted to DOCG status, a theoretically higher status you can read about below, but classification alone doesn't always tell the full story. Bolgheri DOC, for example, has stricter yield controls than some DOCG territories across Italy. Tuscany's current DOC wine count is 41, but this is unlikely to stay the same for long.

DOCG - Denominazione di Origine Controllata e Garantita

DOCG is the highest classification in Italy and applies to wines that meet strict production standards, including lower yields, longer ageing requirements and government-approved tasting panels. Introduced in 1980, this category includes Italy's most prestigious wines, such as Brunello di Montalcino and Chianti Classico. The *Garantita* element ensures the highest level of authenticity, but DOCG wines are not necessarily 'better' than great DOC or IGT wines –

Tenuta Argentiera's Ventaglio vineyard

just more tightly regulated. In Tuscany there are 11 DOCG appellations, which, other than Vernaccia di San Gimignano DOCG, all produce red wine.

IGT - Indicazione Geografica Tipica

Introduced in 1992, the IGT category was a response to the success of wines that didn't fit within DOC rules but were clearly of high quality. IGT wines, such as Toscana IGT, allow for more flexibility in grape varieties and winemaking techniques, making them a playground for innovation. Many high-end Super-Tuscans still use this designation, despite their world-class reputation. Toscana IGT covers the region, and many producers prefer to leverage its brand power in international markets. There are six IGT wines in total.

VdT: Vino da Tavola – Table Wine

Vino da Tavola is the bottom of Italy's wine hierarchy, reserved for basic, everyday wines with no geographical designation. This is typically the kind of wine you'd find on the bottom shelf of supermarkets, sold in cardboard boxes or five-litre plastic bottles. In the 1970s, the category was used by some of Tuscany's most famous estates as a way of producing fine wine from grape varieties not permitted within the traditional DOC system, or from vineyards planted outside traditional appellations. These highly acclaimed wines became known as the Super-Tuscans and challenged consumers to think more deeply about the concept of appellations and the components that make up a fine wine. With the creation of the IGT tier in the 90s, the Vino da Tavola category has mostly returned to its initial role as a vehicle for inexpensive table wine.

Riservas and Superiores

Within the DOC and DOCG categories, additional designations like Superiore and Riserva help distinguish wines of higher quality. These are legally binding terms and indicate stricter production standards, often related to vineyard yields, ageing and alcohol content.

Superiore wines are typically made from lower-yielding vineyards, resulting in greater concentration and structure. They often have slightly higher minimum alcohol levels than their standard counterparts, reflecting riper grapes at harvest. For example, Chianti DOCG *Superiore* must adhere to higher production standards than the standard Chianti DOCG, emphasizing greater depth and body.

Riserva, meanwhile, refers to wines that undergo extended ageing before release. In Tuscany, the exact ageing requirements vary by appellation but typically involve additional time in oak barrels and bottle. Brunello di Montalcino Riserva DOCG, for instance, must age for at least five years, compared to four for Brunello di Montalcino DOCG. This additional ageing allows Riserva wines to develop greater complexity, integrating flavours of oak, spice and tertiary notes like leather and dried fruit.

Both Superiore and Riserva wines are often seen as the flagship expressions of an appellation, embodying its highest quality and stylistic potential. However, they also come with expectations of balance, refinement and the ability to age further. For a long time, that has been mostly true.

Are these labels still relevant?

Historically, time in oak has been equated with quality in Italian wines. Extended ageing in barrel not only adds complexity but also lends structure, finesse and longevity to the wine. It also involves significant costs – oak barrels are expensive, and longer ageing means delayed sales. Traditionally, winemakers reserved their best fruit for wines destined for long maturation, ensuring that Riserva wines, with their additional time in barrel and bottle, commanded a premium and carried a certain prestige.

Similarly, the Superiore designation, often indicating wines with higher alcohol and greater body, aligned with the long-held perception that richness and power equated to quality. For decades, consumers gravitated towards bold, concentrated wines, reinforcing the idea that bigger was better.

However, climate change and shifting consumer preferences are challenging these assumptions. Warmer growing seasons are producing riper fruit naturally, reducing the need for prolonged oak ageing to achieve depth and balance. At the same time, there is growing demand for fresher, more vibrant wines – expressions that emphasize purity of fruit over overt oak influence. As a result, the very definition of quality in Tuscan wine is evolving, leading to a reassessment of traditional classifications.

Recent changes in Italian wine regulations reflect this shift. In Chianti Classico DOCG, the Gran Selezione category was introduced in 2014 (applied from the 2013 vintage) and places an emphasis on estate-grown fruit as a mark of quality. It was refined in 2021 to allow for 11 distinct geographical references (*UGAs - Unità Geografiche Aggiuntive*), a new system that places even greater emphasis on terroir and site-specificity rather than ageing requirements or alcohol levels. The move signals a broader industry trend. Rather than relying on Riserva or Superiore designations to imply quality, producers are now highlighting regional nuances, soil types and microclimates – a return to the idea that where a wine comes from matters as much as how it is made.

While some traditionalists may lament these changes, the reality is that Italian wine classifications have never been static. From the DOCG system's introduction in 1980 to the rise of IGT and Super-Tuscans in response to restrictive DOC rules, the classification system has always adapted to reflect new realities in winemaking and the marketplace.

Bureaucratic decision-making in Italy is notoriously slow, and the country's wine laws are famously complex. Yet history shows that, when change does come, it often serves to reinforce rather than disrupt tradition. The past may dictate many of Italy's rules, but the future will continue to shape how its greatest wines are defined.

Gaiole in Chianti, with Castello di Brolio, right

The wines

You could spend a lifetime studying Tuscan wines. Chianti Classico and Brunello di Montalcino, together, account for thousands of new wines each year. Getting your head around them, and the endless list of producers, is a full-time job. On top of that, there are another nine DOCGs and 41 DOCs to throw into the mix. Don't panic: a little background on the region's most important wines can give you all the basic information you need to rummage with confidence in wine shops and restaurants.

Chianti Classico DOCG

The best place to start is in Chianti, in those famous hills between Florence and Siena. Chianti is one of the best-known wines in the world. That iconic wicker basket flask (the fiasco) was almost everywhere the quintessential accompaniment to spaghetti bolognese. It sat on red-and-white tablecloths in cosy trattorias, and symbolized family and the old country in The Godfather movies. Even Hannibal Lecter enjoyed a bottle. Those were simpler times though, when Chianti was just Chianti, a rustic red wine from Tuscany.

In fact, there are two Chianti appellations. It was in 1716 that Grand Duke Cosimo III de' Medici issued an edict protecting the Chianti territory, which included the villages of Radda, Gaiole, Greve and Castellina. In 1924 the Chianti consortium, taking the black rooster as its symbol (see p18), was founded by 33 producers to protect themselves from imitations and poor quality wines. At the time, Chianti was made from a blend of Sangiovese, complemented by native red grapes like Canaiolo and the white Trebbiano Toscano and Malvasia Bianca.

Controversially, the territory that could legally produce Chianti wines expanded dramatically in 1932, essentially extending the name to red winemaking all over Tuscany. Chianti could then be made from Pisa to Arezzo, Florence to Siena. Style and quality varied. As the decades trundled on, growers in the original 'Classico' area, first defined in 1716, felt the expanded territory was too big. Eventually, they divorced themselves from the wider area and in 1996 Chianti Classico became its own DOCG, governed by its own rules. Since then, the wine has gone from strength to strength. Chianti Classico is not only one of the most important red wines in Italy, it is

Fattoria Fibbiano's 100-year-old Ceppatella vineyard, Terre di Pisa

also one of the most exciting. Few winemaking territories have collectively improved their wines over the last couple of decades and few are so progressively governed.

The wines themselves are vibrant, structured and deeply expressive of Sangiovese's character, with aromas of sour cherry, dried herbs and subtle spice. Modern Chianti Classico strikes a balance between freshness and depth, often having very refined tannins and bright acidity that makes them both food-friendly and age-worthy. There are pronounced stylistic differences based on the village, and of course depending on the approach of individual producers, but the best examples can be outstanding.

In 2014, a new tier to the classification of Chianti Classico was introduced – Gran Selezione. It sits at the top of the appellation's hierarchy and stipulates stricter rules. It requires 100% estate-grown grapes, a minimum of 90% Sangiovese and at least 30 months of ageing, including time in bottle. Stricter vineyard and winemaking standards aim to highlight the region's top expressions, with a focus on terroir-driven quality.

A further move to redefine the way we think about terroir in Chianti Classico came in 2021 as the appellation established the Unità Geografiche Aggiuntive (UGA) system. Similar to MGA (Menzioni Geografiche Aggiuntive) in Barolo, this classification divides Chianti Classico into 11 subzones, each reflecting distinct soil compositions, altitudes – and microclimates. The UGAs – ranging from historic areas like Radda, Gaiole and Castellina to more emergent villages like San Casciano and Panzano – allow producers to indicate a more precise origin on Gran Selezione labels.

Chianti DOCG

After producers in the Classico area secured their own appellation, those outside were left to redefine their identity. Chianti DOCG, established in 1984, was among Italy's first regions to receive DOCG status. However, controlling quality across its vast area proved difficult, leading to the 1996 breakaway of Chianti Classico.

Chianti DOCG encompasses a far-reaching and diverse territory, stretching from Pisa in the west to Arezzo in the east, with numerous subzones contributing to its complexity. The appellation permits references to subzones: Chianti Colli Aretini, Chianti Colli Fiorentini, Chianti Colline Pisane, Chianti Colli Senesi, Chianti Montalbano, Chianti Montespertoli and Chianti Rufina. Each area offers its own expression of Sangiovese, influenced by differences in elevation, climate and soil. While Rufina is known for its bright acidity and structure due to a cooler climate, Colli Senesi often produces softer, more approachable wines.

Unlike Chianti Classico, which follows stricter rules on yields, grape composition and ageing, Chianti DOCG varies widely in style and quality. Some wines are simple, fruit-forward and inexpensive, while others reflect careful craftsmanship and a deep sense of place. One factor contributing to this variability is the allowance of blending with local grape varieties. While Sangiovese remains the dominant grape, producers may include small amounts of traditional Tuscan varieties like Canaiolo and Colorino or even international grapes such as Merlot and Cabernet Sauvignon, depending on local traditions and market preferences. In some subzones, the addition of indigenous grapes helps create wines with a more regional character, enhancing fruit expression, colour or softness.

Tenuta Argentiera winery

For consumers, navigating Chianti DOCG can be challenging. With over 3,000 producers and significant differences between subzones, identifying consistently good wines takes effort. Large-scale cooperative wineries and bulk production contribute to inconsistencies, though dedicated producers continue to craft wines of character and depth, often using traditional winemaking techniques.

Affordability remains a defining trait, with many bottles available for under €10. While lower costs can sometimes reflect uneven quality, those willing to explore will find excellent value. Subzones like Rufina, with its cooler climate, produce some of the most refined and structured examples, offering elegance and longevity at relatively affordable prices.

Ultimately, Chianti DOCG presents both opportunity and challenge. Its diversity ensures a wine for every palate and budget, but understanding subzones, producer reputation and blending practices is key to finding quality within this vast and varied appellation.

Brunello di Montalcino DOCG

In Montalcino, Sangiovese is known as Brunello, and produces wines that are distinct from those found to the north in Chianti territory. The grape has thicker skins and smaller berries, leading to greater concentration and firmer tannins. As a result, Brunello wines can age for decades but require more time to soften in their youth.

Montalcino's warmer climate plays a crucial role in shaping the wine's character. The traditional heartland of production lies on the lower, sun-drenched southern slopes, where warmth and optimal ripening conditions contribute to the appellation's signature power, depth and structure. Here, Sangiovese achieves full maturity with ease, producing intense, long-lived wines. Regulations reflect this ageing potential, requiring at least four years of ageing (and two years in barrel) before release.

However, the territory's expansion over the years has pushed vineyards beyond these prime southern exposures. Today, producers are increasingly looking to the higher-altitude, cooler northern slopes, where a different microclimate offers fresher acidity and greater finesse in the wines. Once considered less favourable for ripening, these northern sites are now gaining importance as rising temperatures make full maturity more achievable in cooler zones. This shift highlights the evolving nature of Brunello di Montalcino, where climate adaptation is playing an ever-growing role in defining style and structure.

The 'modern' version of Brunello di Montalcino was first crafted in the 19th century by Ferruccio Biondi-Santi, who isolated the clone that would become synonymous with the appellation. Brunello quickly gained recognition for its ability to produce wines of exceptional structure and longevity. In 1966 it achieved DOC status, later becoming one of Italy's first DOCG wines in 1980.

Over time, Brunello's production rules have evolved to preserve its integrity and distinctiveness. Regulations mandate that it must be made from 100% Sangiovese, a commitment to purity that sets it apart from other Tuscan appellations. This sanctity was tested during the 2008 blending scandal (see page 27), where several producers were accused of incorporating unauthorized grape varieties to enhance body and colour. The controversy shook confidence but ultimately reinforced the appellation's strict adherence to tradition, with producers doubling down on transparency and authenticity.

Montalcino

The scandal refocused the conversation on terroir. If the sanctity of Sangiovese here was to be respected, then the nuances of site were going to have to come further into the light. The conversation around Brunello's terroir has grown increasingly sophisticated, as winemakers and critics recognize the impact of the region's diverse microclimates. The north-facing slopes, with their cooler temperatures, are known for producing wines with higher acidity and finesse, while the south-facing vineyards benefit from greater sun exposure, creating riper, more robust expressions. These nuances are driving more focused discussions about vineyard site specificity, with some producers advocating for official recognition of subzones within the appellation.

'Rising temperatures challenge the balance of ripeness and acidity that defines classic Brunello'

Climate change has also become a critical issue for Brunello di Montalcino. Rising temperatures are pushing harvests earlier and challenging the balance of ripeness and acidity that defines classic Brunello. These changes have sparked debates about maturation laws, particularly the required ageing periods. Currently, the wine must spend at least two years in oak and a total of four years before release, while Riserva wines require five years of ageing. However, as growing conditions evolve and fruit ripens more fully, many argue that these rigid timelines may no longer be necessary. The push for greater flexibility in maturation rules is gaining traction.

Historically, the area was known for its sweet wines made from the Moscato grape. While the Moscadello di Montalcino appellation still exists, production is now minimal. Far more common is the Rosso di Montalcino DOC, which offers a more approachable alternative. Made from 100% Sangiovese like its prestigious counterpart, it follows a shorter ageing requirement, allowing for fresher, more fruit-driven wines. As a separate DOC, Rosso di Montalcino is produced in smaller quantities and is often seen as a stepping stone to Brunello, providing an earlier-drinking and more affordable expression of Montalcino's terroir.

Vino Nobile di Montepulciano DOCG

Vino Nobile di Montepulciano is made from Prugnolo Gentile, a local clone of Sangiovese, in the historic hilltop town of Montepulciano. Long considered one of Tuscany's great wines, it was once hailed as the 'king of wines' in the 17th century by the Renaissance poet Francesco Redi. While it may not enjoy the same international prestige as Brunello di Montalcino or the marketing power of Chianti Classico, it remains one of the region's most compelling and age-worthy expressions of Sangiovese.

'Vino Nobile is waiting to be rediscovered by those who appreciate great Sangiovese'

The wine is traditionally blended with small amounts of old Tuscan varieties, though in recent years, Cabernet Sauvignon and Merlot have been introduced to add body and softness. The result is a wine that balances ripe cherry and plum flavours with earthy undertones and a touch of spice, framed by firm but approachable tannins. Compared to Brunello, Vino Nobile is typically softer and less structured, favouring elegance over power, while it often has a rounder mouthfeel than Chianti Classico, with oak ageing lending subtle vanilla and cedar notes.

Despite earning DOC status in 1966 and DOCG status in 1980, Vino Nobile di Montepulciano has struggled to command the same prestige as its Tuscan counterparts.

This is partly due to the territory's smaller size and lower production levels, but also, perhaps, because of ongoing confusion with Montepulciano d'Abruzzo, a red wine from an entirely different grape. This misassociation has diluted its identity on the international stage, making it harder for Vino Nobile to distinguish itself despite its deep roots in Tuscan tradition.

The production rules for Vino Nobile allow for a slightly more accessible profile than Brunello di Montalcino. The wines require two years of ageing, with at least one year in oak, compared to Brunello's four-year minimum. This shorter maturation period results in wines that are often ready to drink sooner while still retaining the ability to age for those seeking greater complexity.

Terroir plays a defining role in shaping Vino Nobile's character. The vineyards surrounding Montepulciano benefit from a mix of clay and sandy soils, which contribute to both structure and finesse. The region enjoys a temperate climate, which helps retain acidity and balance in the wines, though, like much of Tuscany, rising temperatures have led to earlier harvests, posing challenges for maintaining freshness.

For those looking for a younger, more approachable expression of Montepulciano's terroir, Rosso di Montepulciano offers an excellent introduction. Made from the same Prugnolo Gentile grape but requiring only a few months of ageing, Rosso is typically fresher, fruitier and designed for earlier drinking, making it an appealing everyday alternative to the more structured Vino Nobile.

While Vino Nobile di Montepulciano may not have the global renown of Brunello or the commercial muscle of Chianti Classico, it occupies a unique middle ground – offering more richness than Chianti but with a more accessible profile than Brunello. It is a wine firmly rooted in Tuscan tradition, waiting to be rediscovered by those who appreciate the depth and elegance of great Sangiovese.

Bolgheri DOC

Bolgheri's rise as a fine wine region is inseparable from the story of Sassicaia, the first Super-Tuscan, a pioneering Bordeaux-style wine that redefined Italian winemaking. In the late 1940s, Mario Incisa della Rocchetta inherited a coastal vineyard and, unimpressed with the quality of Sangiovese in the area, turned his attention to Cabernet Sauvignon and Merlot. His research led him to plant vines on higher-elevation sites overlooking the sea, in rocky soils (sassi in Italian), inspired by the terroirs of Bordeaux. For two decades, Sassicaia was produced privately at Tenuta San Guido, before finally being released commercially in 1971 (1968 vintage), quickly gaining critical acclaim. The success of Sassicaia demonstrated the region's potential for international grape varieties and helped to cement Bolgheri's reputation for excellence.

'Sassicaia was granted its own Bolgheri Sassicaia DOC in 2013'

Initially, Bolgheri's red wines existed outside Italy's traditional appellation system. Early pioneers, including Ornellaia and Guado al Tasso, followed in the footsteps of Sassicaia in the 1970s and 1980s, producing wines from Cabernet Sauvignon, Merlot and Cabernet Franc. Because these wines did not conform to Italy's DOC regulations, they were labelled simply as Vino da Tavola – despite being among the country's most sought-after bottles. This paradox fuelled the Super-Tuscan movement, a term that became synonymous with Bolgheri's high-quality, internationally styled wines.

Bolgheri's terroir is key to its success. The region benefits from a Mediterranean climate, with abundant sunshine, cooling sea breezes and low rainfall during the growing season, which allows for slow and even ripening. Soils vary widely, from sandy and alluvial deposits to clay and limestone, creating ideal conditions for structured, long-lived wines. These factors give Bolgheri reds their hallmark balance of ripeness, freshness and refined tannins.

The region first gained official recognition in 1983 with the creation of the Bolgheri DOC, initially focusing on white and rosé wines. In 1994, the DOC was expanded to include Bolgheri Rosso, formally recognizing the Bordeaux-style red wines that had made the region famous. Within this designation, Bolgheri Superiore represents the highest tier, requiring longer ageing and showcasing greater depth and complexity. Sassicaia's singular status was further reinforced in 2013, when it was granted its own Bolgheri Sassicaia DOC, the only monopole DOC in Italy.

While Bolgheri is best known for its reds, Vermentino has become an increasingly important part of the region's identity. This white grape thrives in the coastal climate, producing crisp, mineral-driven wines that provide a refreshing counterpoint to the powerful reds. As Bolgheri continues to evolve, Vermentino's growing presence highlights the region's versatility and potential beyond its Bordeaux-inspired origins.

Though a relatively young appellation, Bolgheri has quickly secured its place among Italy's most prestigious wine regions. What began as an experiment has become a benchmark for quality, proving that Tuscany's winemaking tradition is as much about innovation as it is about history.

Vernaccia di San Gimignano DOCG

Vernaccia di San Gimignano is Tuscany's most historic white wine and perhaps its most important. Records of Vernaccia, whether as a grape or a wine, first appeared in San Gimignano's tax documents in 1276. Dante Alighieri referenced Vernaccia in *The Divine Comedy*, describing a

Harvest, early morning

pope's atonement for indulging in eels soaked in the wine. Its connection with the medieval town of San Gimignano has endured – whether out of tradition, stubbornness or a deep belief in its potential to produce excellent wines.

Vernaccia di San Gimignano was the first Italian white wine to receive DOC status in 1966. Yet, ironically, it was one of the wines most affected by the agricultural trends of the 1960s and 70s, when high yields and mass production were prioritized over quality. Vernaccia does not respond well to neglect – overcropping results in bland, uninspiring wines.

Gradual improvements followed, and in 1993, Vernaccia di San Gimignano was elevated to DOCG status, reinforcing the push for quality. However, many of the same viticultural challenges remained. Vernaccia requires careful vineyard management year-round to counter its susceptibility to rot in humid conditions and sunburn in hot summers. Keeping yields low is essential, as overcropping leads to neutral, uninspiring wines. In the cellar, Vernaccia presents further challenges. It oxidizes rapidly, and without careful handling, a crisp, fruit-driven wine can quickly develop an undesirable vinegary note.

In recent years, a determined effort – driven in part by the local consortium – has been made to elevate the quality of Vernaccia. This pursuit of excellence has led to a vineyard re-evaluation, where lower yields are now seen as crucial for enhancing fruit expression in this naturally restrained variety. There is now far greater emphasis on lees agitation, which has resulted in wines with a creamier texture and a more complex profile.

The use of oak remains a contentious issue, particularly for delicate varieties like Vernaccia. The DOCG permits a Riserva designation, which requires at least 11 months of ageing before release. Uniquely, producers can select their maturation vessel, but they must decide at harvest whether a wine will be designated as a *Riserva*. Few Italian appellations follow this practice, ensuring that *Riserva* wines are intentionally crafted rather than simply rebranded unsold stock.

This approach makes a strong case for a delicate use of oak. Given Vernaccia's naturally neutral profile, a carefully measured application of wood can add much-needed complexity without overwhelming the wine's freshness. As the region continues to refine its approach, Vernaccia di San Gimignano is proving that Tuscany's great white wine deserves more serious attention.

Vin Santo

Those familiar with Vin Santo appreciate the charming role it plays in Tuscany's food culture. Often brought out after lunch, it is traditionally served with *cantucci* – hard almond biscuits meant to be dipped into the sweet, amber-hued wine. It's a perfect way to linger over an afternoon. Yet, while the tradition of Vin Santo endures, it has increasingly become something of a tourist novelty, with fewer producers committed to maintaining its historic production.

Vin Santo has a long history in Tuscany but traces its origins to the Greek island of Santorini, where sweet wines were made by drying grapes in the sun before pressing them to concentrate sugars. The technique was first imitated by the Venetians and later adopted in Tuscany, where it evolved into a distinctive local style. Today, Trebbiano Toscano and Malvasia Bianca Lunga are the primary grapes used. After harvest, the grapes are dried for several months, often on straw mats or hung in ventilated spaces, allowing sugars to concentrate. The must is then transferred to small wooden barrels known as *caratelli*, where residual yeast (*madre*) from previous batches initiates fermentation. These barrels are sealed and aged for several years, often in attics or cellars where temperature fluctuations contribute to Vin Santo's characteristic depth and complexity. After ageing, the wine is clarified, filtered and bottled, resulting in rich, nutty, honeyed flavours with notes of dried fruit and caramel.

Part of Vin Santo's allure lies in its small-scale production. Few wineries make it today, but it remains an important feature of Tuscan winemaking, particularly in the

Chianti appellations, Carmignano and Montepulciano. Some estates, such as Boscarelli in Montepulciano, maintain old archives of Vin Santo dating back to the 19th century, while others, like the Crociani family, claim to have been maturing it in their cellars since the 14th century.

Even rarer is Occhio di Pernice, a red version of Vin Santo made primarily from Sangiovese. This variation follows the same production method but yields a more intense, spiced profile with dried cherry, fig and tobacco notes, offering a richer, more structured alternative to the classic white style.

The Others

Carmignano DOCG

If only the Carmignano DOCG had a few more wineries. Though not as well known as Tuscany's more prominent appellations, it holds a significant place in Italian wine history. Officially recognized in 1716 by Cosimo III de' Medici, Grand Duke of Tuscany, it is one of the world's oldest delimited wine regions. Granted modern DOCG status in 1990, it showed promise for growth but soon hit a glass ceiling. Despite this, Carmignano remains an appellation worth attention.

By regulation, Carmignano DOCG requires a minimum of 50% Sangiovese, with the option to blend Cabernet Sauvignon and Cabernet Franc, known locally as *Uva Francesca*. This long-standing integration of Bordeaux varieties – dating back centuries – sets Carmignano apart from other Tuscan wines. The result is a style that combines Sangiovese's bright cherry character with Cabernet's structure, depth and notes of dark fruit and spice. Compared to Brunello, Carmignano wines tend to be softer, more approachable and medium-bodied while still retaining freshness.

The vineyards are located just west of Florence in the low Montalbano mountains, where a temperate climate and marl-rich soils provide an ideal environment for balanced ripening.

Hanging Malvasia to dry for Vin Santo, Montepulciano

Terre di Pisa DOC

Terre di Pisa DOC is a relatively new addition to Tuscany's wine conversation. It was established in 2011 and is still very much in its infancy as a wine scene. The area's producers, which as you might suspect extend into the countryside near Pisa, went unnoticed for many years. Most were small, family farms and lacked the resources to participate in territorial marketing campaigns, preferring instead to promote themselves individually. Some might say there hasn't previously been much to market, but regardless, a new generation is starting to communicate internationally about this often ignored part of Tuscany. After all, this is good winemaking territory. Limestone-rich hills ascend steeply from the sea and grapes such as Ciliegiolo and Vermentino provide lots of potential to develop attractive aromatics. There are about a dozen producers worth looking out for and the appellation is a good place to search for value.

Cortona DOC

The town of Cortona, in the south east of the region, has developed a contemporary reputation for Syrah. Also a fairly young appellation, founded in 1999, it is still developing.

That being said, Cortona's affinity with Syrah is one of Italy's viticultural curiosities. With no particularly strong connection to the variety, it is perhaps a reminder that wine regions are still, to some extent, the products of human choice. A handful of wineries, with a personal passion for Rhône Valley varieties, planted Syrah and attempted to differentiate their businesses through it. Producers such as Fabrizio Dionisio have done much to put the town on the region's wine map. Other grapes are grown here too. Sangiovese, Cabernet Sauvignon and Merlot can be found, as well as the very fragrant Malvasia Nera. White wines are produced mainly with Chardonnay and Sauvignon Blanc.

Morellino di Scansano DOCG

Morellino di Scansano is another of Tuscany's Sangiovese expressions. It is located in the broader coastal Maremma area, and has been recognized as a DOCG since 2007. The appellation, which markets itself as *Sangiovese by the sea*, benefits from a Mediterranean climate where warm days and cooling breezes create wines with vibrant fruit, supple tannins and fresh acidity.

The name 'Morellino' reflects local tradition, with some linking it to the dark-coated Morello horses of the region. The wines must contain at least 85% Sangiovese, often blended with Ciliegiolo or Merlot, which add floral, red cherry and wild herb notes. Morellino di Scansano is typically made in a youthful, fruit-driven style, though a Riserva version requires at least two years of ageing, including one in oak, lending it greater depth and structure.

Unlike Chianti Classico or Brunello, Morellino di Scansano was historically a farmer's wine, made for local consumption rather than international prestige. In the early days of the appellation, growers lacked a clear vision of the style they wanted to present to the world, resulting in wines that sometimes felt incoherent. But in recent years, Morellino di Scansano has become more defined, recognized as a softer, more fragrant take on Sangiovese. With its powerful, sun-kissed profile and coastal freshness, it is now firmly establishing its identity as Maremma's signature red.

The best Tuscan vintages of the last 30 years

As with any great wine region, vintages vary. Beyond the simple description of warmer and cooler years, the differences can be subtle, with the nuances of the growing season only noticeable in the glass after several years.

Franco Biondi-Santi, who died in 2013, with a bottle of 1888

There isn't much very old Tuscan wine in circulation, but the vintages below have proved themselves to be outstanding, and top producers still demonstrate this with regular releases from their libraries of wine. Although overall vintage character tends to be consistent across the region, microclimates can affect vineyards in different ways, so following the work of individual producers is still the best approach. As the climate continues to change, Tuscany's various wine territories are at risk of rising temperatures and freak weather. Winemakers are quickly adapting in search of freshness and balance, but can do little about sudden frosts, extreme drought or major downpours of rain and hail. The business of growing grapes remains at the mercy of nature; uncertainty and unpredictability are part of the magic of wine.

The best Tuscan vintages of the last 30 years

1997

A warm, dry growing season resulted in concentrated, ripe wines with great depth. Particularly strong in Chianti Classico, Brunello di Montalcino and Bolgheri, this vintage helped put Super-Tuscans on the global map.

1999

A problematic vintage that turned out well in the end. A balanced growing season produced wines with excellent structure, freshness and ageing potential. Brunello di Montalcino and Chianti Classico excelled, showing refined tannins and long-term promise.

2001

A cool start followed by a warm summer led to wines of finesse and complexity. Rains hit in September, but what's still around is often well balanced with good fruit and acidity still. Time has proven 2001 to be exceptional in Brunello di Montalcino and Vino Nobile di Montepulciano. Delivering structured but elegant wines built for ageing.

2004

Consistently warm but not overly hot, this vintage produced classically structured wines with freshness and longevity. Brunello di Montalcino and Chianti Classico were particularly strong, with vibrant acidity and well-defined tannins.

2006

A warm but balanced season resulted in robust, intense wines with strong tannins and ageing potential. Best in Brunello di Montalcino, Chianti Classico Riserva and Bolgheri, where wines showed remarkable depth and structure.

'2016 is considered one of the best vintages in recent history'

2010

A nearly perfect vintage, producing balanced, long-lived wines with precision and elegance. Outstanding in Brunello di Montalcino, Chianti Classico and Bolgheri, with many wines developing beautifully over time.

2015

A warm year with plenty of sun yielded ripe, concentrated wines with plush fruit and firm structure. Excellent for Brunello di Montalcino and Bolgheri, producing powerful, expressive wines with deep complexity.

2016

Widely considered one of the best in recent history, with ideal growing conditions leading to fresh, vibrant and perfectly balanced wines. Standout performances in Brunello di Montalcino, Chianti Classico and Bolgheri, with wines showing remarkable clarity, energy and age-worthiness.

10 wines to look out for

To suggest a handful of wines out of the thousands of treasures that Tuscany offers is an almost impossible task. This list of ten memorable wines is simply a way of getting you started.

The barrel cellar at Il Borro, Valdarno di Sopra

Inevitably, the Super-Tuscans come with premium prices, but they help illuminate Tuscany's contemporary wine revolution, and its importance internationally. Other choices are more accessible, but just as symbolic of their respective territories. We would encourage you to pair these wines with local dishes: they'll be beautiful in the glass, and worthy of sipping and savouring by themselves, but they reach a new level with a thoughtful food pairing. Is there anything more appealing than the moreish, savoury texture of Chianti Classico, with its fragrance of black cherry and violets, paired with a matured and perfectly-cooked Florentine steak? We haven't listed vintages – refer to The best Tuscan vintages of the last 30 years (see pp78–81), or go with the vintage that is the winery's current release.

Tenuta Tignanello, Tignanello, Toscana IGP

One of Italy's most influential wines, pioneering the Super-Tuscan movement. Produced under the Toscana IGP designation, it blends Sangiovese with Cabernet Sauvignon and Cabernet Franc, breaking the once traditional Chianti Classico rules. Aged in barriques, it is known for its depth, structure and ageing potential, redefining modern Tuscan winemaking.

Tenuta San Guido, Sassicaia, Bolgheri Sassicaia DOC

Tenuta San Guido 'Sassicaia' is Italy's most iconic Super-Tuscan, the first to prove that Bordeaux varieties could thrive in Tuscany. Made primarily from Cabernet Sauvignon, with Cabernet Franc, it set the standard for Bolgheri's wines and inspired the development of the territory. Aged in French oak, it is renowned for its elegance, complexity and longevity – and comes with a lofty price tag.

Le Macchiole, Bolgheri Rosso, Bolgheri DOC

A lesser-known yet pioneering wine from one of Bolgheri's most respected estates. A blend of Merlot, Cabernet Sauvignon, Cabernet Franc and Syrah, it showcases the region's potential for fresh, elegant wines with a strong sense of place. Structured yet vibrant, it reflects Bolgheri's evolving identity.

Biondi-Santi, Brunello di Montalcino, Tenuta Greppo, Brunello di Montalcino DOCG

Credited with defining the style in the 19th century, Biondi-Santi Tenuta Greppo has the reputation of producing the original Brunello. Made exclusively from Sangiovese, it is known for its elegant, ethereal power and exceptional longevity. A benchmark for traditional Brunello, it remains one of Italy's most historic and collectible wines.

Castellare di Castellina, Chianti Classico Riserva, Chianti Classico DOCG

A classic expression of Sangiovese, with a small percentage of Canaiolo. Cultivated at around 400m in limestone soils, it is aged in oak, this Riserva still consistently has bright acidity, firm tannins and layered complexity. It's a classic wine, deeply rooted in tradition and still a benchmark for the appellation.

Boscarelli, Il Nocio, Vino Nobile di Montepulciano DOCG

Boscarelli's Il Nocio is only made in small quantities, but as a single-vineyard expression of 100% Prugnolo, it's one of Montepulciano's best red wines. Aged in oak, its refined tannins, bright acidity and complex red fruit and spice notes make it a perfect accompaniment to classic Tuscan menus.

Querciabella, Batàr, Toscana IGP

A blend of Chardonnay and Pinot Bianco, Batàr is one of Tuscany's most distinctive white wines. Grown in the hills close to Greve in Chianti, the grapes are fermented and aged in French oak, giving the wine texture, depth and ageing potential. Rich and layered, with notes of ripe stone fruit, almond and subtle spice, Batàr has long been considered a reference point for the region and is frequently compared with white Burgundy.

Grattamacco Vermentino, Bolgheri DOC

Grattamacco's Vermentino is grown on limestone-rich soils at around 100-200m above sea level in the hills overlooking the Tyrrhenian coast. Fermented in stainless steel with partial skin contact, it is consistently a textured, saline style of the variety that balances intense aromas with depth and concentration. Notes of citrus peel, wild herbs and white flowers are supported by a mineral backbone, making it one of the best examples of coastal Tuscan white wine.

Petrolo, Bòggina B Trebbiano, Toscana IGP

Made from 100% Trebbiano Toscano, Bòggina B comes from the Valdarno di Sopra area near Arezzo, specifically from the Bòggina vineyard at around 300m above sea level. Fermented with native yeasts and aged in French oak tonneaux, it shows the depth and ageing potential of Trebbiano when carefully handled. With notes of stone fruit, chamomile and subtle spice, this is a structured and textural white wine that reflects both site and variety. It is quietly becoming a cult wine for Italian wine collectors.

Il Colombaio di Santa Chiara, Riserva L'Albereta, Vernaccia di San Gimignano DOCG

Sourced from a single vineyard near San Gimignano, L'Albereta is made from 100% Vernaccia di San Gimignano grapes cultivated organically. The wine undergoes fermentation with indigenous yeasts in oak barrels, followed by 12 months of ageing – 70% in oak and 30% in concrete vats. This low-production Riserva is a golden yellow in the glass, with seductive aromas of apricot and brioche. It is one of the more interesting expressions of Tuscany's most historical white wine.

Grape skins in the vat after fermentation,
Tenuta Guado al Tasso

San Felice: timeless Tuscan wine and hospitality

Nestled in the heart of Chianti Classico, near the historic village of Castelnuovo Berardenga, the **San Felice Winery** stands as an example of Tuscany's rich viticultural heritage.

Both respectful of tradition as well as looking forward to the future, San Felice offers the highest-quality wines and an immersive and luxurious visitor experience.

Our philosophy is rooted in sustainability, scientific research and the protection of indigenous grape varieties: our pioneering **Vitiarium** project, for example, preserves and studies over 250 ancient Tuscan grape varieties.

The wines of San Felice, from 155ha of vineyards enriched by mineral-rich soils on gently rolling hills, are a true reflection of the Chianti terroir. Our flagship wine, **Il Grigio Chianti Classico Riserva**, a powerful and elegant Sangiovese, pays homage to the region's noble winemaking traditions. Equally notable is **Poggio Rosso**, a single-vineyard Chianti Classico Gran Selezione, celebrated for its depth, structure and ageing potential.

Then there is the **Vitiarium** collection, four distinct labels designed for high-end dining: **Borgo Chianti Classico DOCG**, **La Pieve Chianti Classico DOCG Gran Selezione**, **Pugnitello Toscana IGT** and **In Avane Chardonnay Toscana IGT**.

For wine lovers and travellers, San Felice offers far more than bottles to be admired. The estate is home to the Relais & Châteaux **Borgo San Felice**, a medieval village transformed into a luxurious resort, with cobbled streets, stone houses and breathtaking views of the vineyards and olive groves.

Visitors can taste the range of wines at the **Enoteca**, explore the estate on guided vineyard walks and take cooking classes that celebrate Tuscan culinary traditions. At the end of the day, unwind at the wellness centre or take a dip in the panoramic pool.

We have two internationally-renowned restaurants, run by chef Juan Quintero in collaboration with Michelin-starred chef Enrico Bartolini. The Michelin-starred (and Michelin Green Star 2023) **Poggio Rosso*** is an intimate and sophisticated gourmet restaurant, complemented by the traditional Tuscan family atmosphere of **Osteria Il Grigio.**

San Felice's vision is holistic. This isn't just a winery, but a living testament to Tuscan culture, which blends agriculture, hospitality, sustainability and research into one harmonious experience.

Whether you're sipping a glass of Sangiovese at sunset, or strolling vineyards that have been tended for centuries, a visit to San Felice leaves a lasting impression of elegance, authenticity and the timeless allure of the Chianti Classico countryside.

Visiting Tuscany

When is the best time to visit Tuscany? It might be the quiet of winter, when the scent of woodsmoke wafts through the villages, or high summer, when town squares teem with life till the early hours – or maybe you prefer to arrange your trip around one of the great Tuscan festivals?

The Palio, Siena

When to visit

Spring

In spring, the season of renewal, Tuscan vineyards wake from their winter sleep and wildflowers spill across the hills. The weather can be beautifully mild, but the region gets its fair share of rain, which explains Tuscany's lush, green landscapes. This is a great time to be out in nature, walking through vineyard rows or exploring the countryside as it bursts back to life. The towns and villages prepare for summer, tables and chairs reappear in the piazzas and seasonal ingredients like asparagus and artichokes make their way onto menus. It's a time of energy and anticipation, before the full heat of summer arrives.

Summer

As visitors fill the region, key attractions get crowded. The heat can be intense, encouraging a slower pace among the locals, who emerge later at night to fill the trattorias and wine bars. It's a lively season, with a programme of festivals and open-air concerts taking place in most towns, bringing a civilized energy to the evenings. The roads are still busy, not just with cars but also with cyclists making the most of the long daylight hours to tackle the hills. In the vineyards, the vines start to hang heavy with fruit, making this the most evocative time to be visiting.

Autumn

Autumn in Tuscany is defined by harvest and abundance, as vineyards buzz with activity, and the scent of fermenting grapes drifts through the air. The countryside turns to deep gold and rust, and the markets overflow with truffles, porcini mushrooms and freshly pressed olive oil. Wineries open their doors for harvest tours, offering the rare chance to see winemaking in progress. In restaurants, game dishes return, paired with the first pours of newly released wines (known as the *annata* wines). With the summer crowds thinning, cooler temperatures and softer light, this is a very atmospheric time to explore Tuscany's wine and food culture.

Winter

Winter in Tuscany is quiet. The vineyards are dormant, and the hills often veiled in soft mist. The roads are emptier, making it easier to explore without the usual crowds, though many cafés and restaurants close in January, particularly in smaller towns. In the countryside, the scent of woodsmoke drifts through the air, and the warmth of a fireplace-lit trattoria offers the perfect setting for hearty Tuscan dishes – slow-cooked stews, ribollita soup and rich game meats. Though the landscape is bare, winter sunshine is frequent, casting a golden light over the stone villages and making this an unexpectedly beautiful time to visit.

The town of Volterra in winter

Festivals

Tuscany's most important festivals can be religious, gastronomic or vinous – or indeed all three. Calici di Stelli (see below) is a nationwide initiative that opens up some of the best wineries, but there are plenty of highly localized events that are worth looking out for. Given that most Tuscans decamp to the beach for the summer, many of the best culinary festivals fall off-season.

Palio di Siena (July & August)

The Palio di Siena is a centuries-old Tuscan tradition. Held twice a year, in July and August, this bareback horse race takes place in the Piazza del Campo, where Siena's 17 contrade (districts) fiercely compete for victory. The atmosphere is electric, with flag-waving parades, medieval costumes and passionate locals. Access to the piazza is free for everyone, so arrive early and bring water. Once you're in, you can't leave until it's finished.

thepalio.eu/the-palio/

Calici di Stelli (August)

A highlight of the Tuscan summer is Calici di Stelle ('glasses of stars'). Held on warm summer nights in August, it's a nationwide initiative that brings wine lovers together to drink under the night sky. Organized by the Movimento Turismo del Vino Toscana, the event sees participating

Calici di Stelli

wineries across Tuscany open their doors for special tastings, vineyard dinners and live music, creating an unforgettable setting for enjoying wine outdoors. From medieval piazzas to rural estates, each location offers a unique backdrop to experience Tuscany's wines in their natural setting. With meteor showers often coinciding with the event, the magic of the night sky only enhances the atmosphere.

mtvtoscana.com/
movimentoturismovino.it/calici-di-stelle-3/

Bravìo delle Botti (August)

Every year, on the last Sunday of August, Montepulciano's *Bravìo delle Botti* turns the town's steep, cobbled streets into a stage for one of Tuscany's most gruelling yet exhilarating contests. Teams from the eight *contrade* (districts) push 80-kg wine barrels uphill for 1,800 metres, battling through sharp turns and ancient alleyways in a test of endurance, precision and local pride. The prize is the Panno, a hand-painted banner dedicated to San Giovanni Decollato, Montepulciano's patron saint. Originally a 14th-century horse race, the Bravìo was revived in 1974, replacing horses with barrels to honour the town's winemaking heritage. Expect pageantry, parades and fierce competition – Tuscany at its most theatrical.

braviodellebotti.com/

Chianti Classico Expo (September)

Held annually in Greve in Chianti, the Chianti Classico Expo is a rare opportunity to explore the region's wines in one place. With over 300 producers making Chianti Classico, understanding the appellation's diversity can be overwhelming. This event simplifies that challenge, bringing together a broad selection of wineries for guided tastings, cultural events and direct interactions with winemakers. The experience is both educational and sensory – you'll notice the subtle differences between producers while appreciating the remarkable consistency in quality across the region. Hosted in Piazza Matteotti, this is one of the best ways to discover new wineries and deepen your understanding of Sangiovese's expression in Chianti Classico.

expochianticlassico.com/en/

Chianti Classico Expo

Volterragusto (October)

Set against the medieval backdrop of Volterra, Volterra Gusto is a celebration of the region's food, wine and handicrafts. The festival's highlight is Volterra's prized white truffle, harvested in the surrounding hills and showcased through tastings, cooking demonstrations and market stalls. Alongside truffles, visitors can sample local olive oils, cheeses and wines, including selections from nearby producers within appellations like Chianti DOCG and Bolgheri DOC. The event also promotes Volterra's artisanal heritage, with exhibitions of ceramics and alabaster craftsmanship. With live music, guided tastings and a lively market atmosphere, Volterra Gusto offers an authentic taste of Tuscany in autumn.

volterragusto.com/

The squid festival of Capraia (October/November)

Held each autumn on the island of Capraia, the Sagra del Totano marks the start of the squid-fishing season with a weekend of maritime tradition, food and festivities. The highlight is the squid-fishing competition, where teams compete to catch the largest or most squid, but for visitors, the real draw is the food – a celebration of Tuscan coastal cuisine, featuring squid-based risottos, stews and fritti,

The squid festival of Capraia

all paired with local wines. With its lively atmosphere and stunning island setting, the Capraia Squid Festival gives a rare glimpse into the culinary traditions of one of Tuscany's most remote outposts.

sagradeltotano.it/

National White Truffles Exhibition in San Miniato (November)

Held over multiple weekends in November, the National White Truffle Exhibition of San Miniato is one of Tuscany's most important culinary events, celebrating the region's prized tuber magnatum pico. San Miniato's unique microclimate and forested hills produce some of Italy's finest white truffles, which take centre stage at this bustling market. Visitors can taste and purchase fresh truffles, sample truffle-infused dishes and explore local wines, cheeses and cured meats. The event also features cooking demonstrations, pairings and artisan markets.

terredipisa.it/en/events/national-white-truffle-fair-san-miniato/

The towns

Amidst the grandeur of medieval and Renaissance architecture, Tuscany's towns and cities pulse with the chaotic rhythm of modern Italian life and the steady flow of tourism.

Sunlit piazzas fill with café chatter, market stalls are full of seasonal produce and vespas dart through streets crowded with visitors. The contrast is part of the appeal. Historic *enotecas* serve wines shaped by centuries of tradition, and butchers carve *bistecca* with theatrical flair. And just beyond the town walls, vineyards, olive groves and forests stretch towards the horizon.

Montepulciano

Florence

Florence may be Tuscany's cultural heart, but it is also a city shaped by food and wine. For all its Renaissance treasures, the daily rituals of eating and drinking remain central to its identity. Exploring them, however, requires navigating the tourist-heavy streets and knowing where to look.

The city's historic enotecas are a good place to start. Le Volpi e l'Uva, near Ponte Vecchio, is one of Florence's best wine bars, specializing in small, independent Tuscan producers, while Casa del Vino, tucked behind the bustling San Lorenzo market, pairs wines by the glass with local charcuterie and cheese. The city's *buchette del vino*, small Renaissance-era wine windows once used by merchants to sell directly to the public, have been restored in recent years, offering a uniquely Florentine way to enjoy a glass of wine on the go.

Morning is the best time to experience Florence before the crowds take over. A quiet espresso at Caffè Gilli or Ditta Artigianale offers a moment of calm before exploring the city's famous landmarks, such as the Duomo, Ponte Vecchio and the Uffizi gallery. Those looking for a deeper dive into Florentine food culture should make their way to Mercato

di Sant'Ambrogio, the city's most authentic market, where locals shop for fresh produce, meat and wine. For a quick lunch, All'Antico Vinaio is famous for its panini, but smaller sandwich shops around Via dei Cimatori offer equally good alternatives with less fanfare.

For those interested in wine beyond Chianti, the Oltrarno district provides a more artisanal side to Florence's drinking culture. Wine bars here focus on lesser-known appellations such as Carmignano and Chianti Rufina, offering an alternative to the predictable lists found in more tourist-heavy areas. In the early evening, Procacci is a refined spot for a glass of Super-Tuscan wine alongside its famous truffle panini.

Dinner in Florence inevitably leads to *bistecca alla Fiorentina*, best enjoyed at classic establishments like Trattoria Cammillo or Osteria Vini e Vecchi Sapori. For those wanting to explore wine at the highest level, Enoteca Pinchiorri, with one of Europe's most extensive cellars, is an essential stop. Florence rewards those who take the time to look past the surface. For wine and food lovers, it is a city that reveals itself slowly, through its markets, enotecas and the centuries-old relationship between its streets and the vineyards beyond.

Siena

Siena's medieval streets, lined with Gothic and Renaissance architecture, wind their way towards the iconic Piazza del Campo, one of the most famous squares in Italy. Twice a year, this semicircular piazza transforms into the stage for the Palio, a fiercely contested horse race dating back to 1633, where tradition, rivalry and pageantry collide in a breathtaking spectacle.

Throughout the summer Siena is busy, with many of the cafés and restaurants feeling quite touristy. Even so, there are lots of opportunities to eat and drink well a stone's throw from the soaring Torre del Mangia.

Despite the inevitable queues during peak season, Siena retains its unmistakable Tuscan character, offering a balance of history, culture and gastronomy. While most bars and restaurants feature a list of local wines, a select few elevate the experience with expertly curated selections and knowledgeable service. La Taverna di San Giuseppe, set within a 13th century cellar, is a standout for its traditional dishes like hand-rolled pici with wild boar ragù, paired with aged Chianti Classico Riserva. Osteria Le Logge, just steps from Piazza del Campo, takes a more refined approach, offering a sommelier-led wine list alongside regional specialities. Osteria Il Carroccio, known for its welcoming atmosphere, has a strong focus on Sienese flavours, from *cinta senese* pork to classic *peposo* stew.

For those using Siena as a base to explore Tuscany, staying just outside the historic city walls offers a balance of tranquility and convenience. One excellent option is La Certosa di Maggiano, a former monastery turned boutique retreat, blending contemporary style with historic charm. The property features its own highly regarded wine cellar and a fine dining restaurant, making it an ideal choice for food and wine lovers. Its location provides easy access to Siena's vibrant centre and to the surrounding countryside, where some of Tuscany's most celebrated wineries await.

The vineyards around Siena span a broad spectrum of styles, from the iconic estates of Chianti Classico to the Vernaccia-producing wineries of San Gimignano and the structured reds of Montepulciano. A short drive south leads to the Brunello heartland of Montalcino, where producers like Biondi-Santi, Casanova di Neri and Poggio di Sotto craft some of Italy's most sought-after wines. Whether enjoying a casual glass in an enoteca, a formal tasting at a historic estate or a meal expertly paired with Tuscan wines, Siena offers an unforgettable journey through the region's wine and culinary heritage.

Siena

Pisa

Pisa is a lively student city that, in summer, fills with day-trippers, most making a brief stop at the Leaning Tower before moving on. The area around Piazza dei Miracoli, where the Duomo and Baptistery stand, is the busiest, but beyond this, the city offers plenty to those willing to explore.

Pisa

For a quieter, more local experience, a walk towards Borgo Stretto is a must. This medieval street, lined with porticoes, is home to some of Pisa's best cafés and pastry shops. Pasticceria Salza, a historic bakery, is known for its *Torta coi Bischeri*, a chocolate and pine nut tart typical of the city. For wine lovers, Enoteca Bacchus serves a well-curated selection of Tuscan wines by the glass, including a few bottles from the local Terre di Pisa DOC, an appellation still defining its identity but increasingly visible in the city's enotecas.

Across the Arno River, the San Martino district feels more residential, with small trattorias and wine bars tucked into its side streets. Osteria di Culegna is a good place to try *baccalà alla pisana* (salt cod with tomato and pine nuts), while Ristoro Pisano offers heartier Tuscan dishes and a short but well-chosen wine list. Pisa's food culture also leans towards the coast, and *cecina*, a simple but satisfying chickpea flatbread, is a local favourite often found in bakeries and pizzerias.

Beyond food and wine, Pisa rewards those who explore its quieter streets. The Palazzo Blu, a cultural hub along the Arno, hosts rotating exhibitions covering everything from Renaissance art to modern photography. Nearby, Piazza dei Cavalieri is a striking square, once home to the Knights of St Stephen, and now dominated by the grand façade of the Scuola Normale Superiore, one of Italy's most prestigious universities. For those looking to escape the crowds altogether, the Orto e Museo Botanico, one of Europe's oldest botanical gardens, offers a peaceful retreat just minutes from the city centre. It's a useful spot for shaking off the effects of the night before.

Pisa is often compared to Florence as a smaller, more navigable open-air museum, but it's best appreciated as a place for unhurried wandering. Between its historic cafés, vibrant markets and cultural sites, it offers plenty to discover for those willing to look beyond its most famous landmark.

Lucca

Just a short trip from Pisa, Lucca is a walled city with a compact yet surprisingly spacious historic centre. Unlike many Tuscan towns, its Renaissance-era walls remain fully intact, now serving as a tree-lined promenade that circles the city. While Lucca lacks the international fame of Florence or Siena, it has a strong local identity, with its food and traditions at the heart of daily life.

Wine is not a major attraction here, but the surrounding Colline Lucchesi hills are home to a handful of small winemaking farms, producing Sangiovese-based reds and fresh, mineral-driven whites. Fattoria di Fubbiano and Tenuta di Valgiano are among the most respected producers, offering tastings just a short drive from the city centre.

The Lucchese take great pride in their local delicacies, and *buccellato* is the most iconic. This sweet, anise-flavoured bread, often studded with raisins, is a staple in Lucca's bakeries, with Taddeucci near Piazza San Michele being the best-known spot to try it. The city's trattorias and osterias serve rustic Tuscan cuisine, with standouts like *Tordelli Lucchesi*, a stuffed pasta similar to ravioli, traditionally filled with meat and herbs.

Lucca is best explored at a slow pace, whether wandering its narrow alleys, cycling its walls or enjoying a long meal at a piazza-side café. While it may not be a major wine destination, its food culture and relaxed atmosphere make it an essential stop in northern Tuscany.

San Gimignano

San Gimignano's 14 medieval towers, standing high above its well-preserved stone walls, reflect an era when powerful families competed to build ever-taller structures as symbols of status and influence. Today, they stand as both an architectural spectacle and a reminder of the town's medieval affluence – one that also extended to its winemaking traditions, particularly Vernaccia di San

Gimignano, a white wine with a history dating back to 1296. Unlike the Sangiovese dominance of nearby Chianti, Vernaccia has shaped San Gimignano's identity for centuries. It was referenced by Dante in *The Divine Comedy*, became Italy's first DOC wine in 1966, and was later upgraded to DOCG status in 1993. Once dismissed as a simple wine, Vernaccia has moved towards more structured, mineral-driven expressions, with leading producers refining their styles. Visitors interested in exploring this evolution can stop at the Consorzio-run Wine Experience in the town centre.

Though Vernaccia dominates, San Gimignano DOC reds – historically overshadowed by Chianti – are improving. Producers are refining their Sangiovese-based blends, incorporating Cabernet Sauvignon and Merlot to craft richer, more structured wines. The surrounding 730 hectares of vineyards reflect this gradual shift, with more estates adding red wines alongside their Vernaccia production.

San Gimignano is one of Tuscany's most visited towns, with around two million visitors a year, but the crowds ease in the evenings, revealing a more relaxed side to its food and wine culture. Bel Soggiorno and Le Vecchie Mura, two of the town's more traditional restaurants, offer classic Tuscan dishes like *ribollita* and *cinghiale alla vernaccia* (wild boar cooked in Vernaccia wine). For a broader tasting experience, Enoteca DiVinorum curates a strong selection of Vernaccia, including much-improved Riservas, alongside local meats and cheeses.

San Gimignano

Beyond food and wine, San Gimignano rewards unhurried exploration. The Collegiata di Santa Maria Assunta, with its frescoes by Ghirlandaio, gives a glimpse into the town's artistic heritage, while a short climb to the Rocca di Montestaffoli provides panoramic views over the vineyards and rolling countryside. These landscapes have shaped the town's wines for generations, but for visitors today, they feel like classic Tuscan vistas and the reason you're there.

Montalcino

The roads leading to Montalcino climb steeply through a landscape of vineyards, olive groves and dense woodland, reinforcing the town's position as a natural stronghold. Historically, this elevated perch made it a fortress town of strategic importance, but today its significance lies in Brunello di Montalcino, one of Italy's most revered wines. Unlike Tuscany's busier destinations, Montalcino, in the south of the region, sees fewer but more deliberate visitors – wine enthusiasts, history lovers and those drawn to its slower rhythm.

Montalcino's devotion to Brunello is immediately apparent. Bottle shops and Brunello-focused restaurants line the streets, interspersed with a handful of artisanal stores selling Tuscan linens, ceramics and olive oil. The fortress, built in 1361, now houses an enoteca where visitors can experience wines from older vintages within its historic walls. Climbing its towers provides sweeping views of the Val d'Orcia, a reminder that Montalcino was once the last bastion of the Republic of Siena before it fell to Florence.

If you're in a hurry, a half day would suffice. The town itself is compact, centred around Piazza del Popolo and the main street through the town. The Palazzo dei Priori, a 13th century town hall with its slender clock tower, dominates the square, while the Chiesa di Sant'Agostino and Museo Civico e Diocesano reflect Montalcino's medieval past and its role as both a religious and civic centre.

Outside the town walls, hundreds of wineries produce Brunello and Rosso di Montalcino DOC, a younger, more approachable wine made from Sangiovese but aged for less time. There are now over 200 producers here, and most offer tours and tastings, which you need to book in advance. Certain names stand out: Biondi-Santi, who were instrumental in the creation of Brunello, is a must-visit; Poggio Antico, with the highest vineyards in the appellation; and Casanova di Neri and Poggio di Sotto, who also produce highly regarded, premium wines.

The quality of nearby Sant'Antimo DOC wines has also risen in recent years. The vineyards in the countryside south of Montalcino produce reds and whites under the appellation named after the Abbazia di Sant'Antimo, one of Tuscany's most atmospheric landmarks. The abbey's Romanesque architecture, soft travertine stone and tranquil setting among cypress trees make it an evocative stop.

For lunch, Osteria di Porta al Cassero is a well-loved spot serving traditional Montalcinese dishes in a warm, unpretentious setting – ideal for long, relaxed meals with liver and mushroom crostini, wild boar stew and a bottle of Brunello.

Whether sipping Brunello at an enoteca, taking in the view from the fortress or visiting Sant'Antimo's peaceful valley, Montalcino offers a slower, more immersive experience of Tuscany, where wine and history remain inseparably linked.

Montepulciano

The hilltop town of Montepulciano, just east of Montalcino, is known for its Renaissance architecture, panoramic views and deep historical significance. Sitting atop a ridge between the Val d'Orcia and the Val di Chiana, it is a crucial destination for those seeking a blend of art, history and wine. Montepulciano is synonymous with Vino Nobile di Montepulciano, one of Tuscany's most prestigious wines, produced primarily from Prugnolo Gentile, a local Sangiovese clone.

Celebrated since the 16th century, Vino Nobile is known for its elegance, structure and ageing potential. Many wineries, both in the surrounding countryside and within the town, offer tastings. Historic cellars beneath ancient palazzi, such as Cantina Contucci and De' Ricci, provide an atmospheric backdrop to the wine culture here. Montepulciano is also home to Vin Santo di Montepulciano, a traditional dessert wine made from dried grapes, aged in attic barrels to develop its distinctive nutty and honeyed character.

At the heart of the town, Piazza Grande is surrounded by Renaissance and medieval buildings. The Palazzo Comunale, with its clock tower inspired by Florence's Palazzo Vecchio, dominates the square, affording panoramic views for those who reach the top. Nearby, the Cathedral of Santa Maria Assunta houses Taddeo di Bartolo's The Assumption of the Virgin, while the Chiesa di Sant'Agostino and the Museo Civico e Diocesano provide further insight into Montepulciano's religious and artistic heritage.

Montepulciano's cultural identity is also tied to its humanist past. The poet and scholar Angelo Poliziano, a prominent figure in the Medici court, was born here, and his legacy is woven into the town's intellectual traditions. Each summer, the Cantiere Internazionale d'Arte brings together musicians and artists, reflecting the town's enduring role as a centre of creativity. Another local tradition is the *Bravio delle Botti*, a barrel-rolling race held in late August, where athletes from the town's eight districts push heavy barrels uphill to Piazza Grande, accompanied by parades and celebrations.

For dining, La Grotta, near the San Biagio Church, is exceptionally good for seasonal Tuscan dishes like truffle-infused *pici pasta* and *bistecca alla Fiorentina*, paired with an excellent Vino Nobile selection. Osteria Acquacheta offers a rustic, convivial experience, known for its grilled steaks and hearty Tuscan menu. Beyond restaurants, expect all the usual artisanal food shops selling regional specialities, from pecorino cheese and olive oil, to honey and handmade pasta.

A short drive from Montepulciano leads to Sant'Antimo, Chiusi and Pienza. Chiusi, once an important Etruscan city, features an Etruscan Museum and the Labyrinth of Porsenna, a vast underground network of tunnels. Pienza, designed by Pope Pius II as the 'ideal Renaissance city', offers harmonious architecture, Val d'Orcia views and a reputation for exceptional Pecorino cheese.

Montepulciano

Bolgheri

Once an agricultural backwater, Bolgheri has transformed itself into one of Italy's most prestigious wine towns, producing some of the country's most sought-after and highly priced wines. On the Tuscan coast, south of Livorno and just north of the historic Etruscan port of Piombino, the area is best known for its Bordeaux-style reds – the famed Super-Tuscans – made from Cabernet and Merlot. They are a stark contrast to the Sangiovese-dominated wines made inland.

Despite its global reputation, Bolgheri itself is a small village, more of a hub for wine lovers than a major urban centre. Its medieval Castello di Bolgheri and cobbled streets lined with wine shops and cafés make for a pleasant stop, but the real attraction is beyond its walls – the wineries that have redefined Tuscan winemaking. Some of Italy's most iconic estates, including Ornellaia and Le Macchiole, produce exceptional wines here, blending international grape varieties in the region's unique coastal climate.

For many visitors, the journey to Bolgheri is just as captivating as the wines themselves. The famous Viale dei Cipressi, a 5km road lined with over 2,500 cypress trees, creates one of Tuscany's most striking approaches. Originally planted in the early 19th century by the Counts of Gherardesca, the road was immortalized in Giosuè Carducci's poem *Davanti a San Guido*. Those with time should consider cycling or running along this stunning stretch before heading into town. Beginning at the San Guido estate near the Via Aurelia, an ancient Roman road, it stretches in a straight line towards the town walls.

A visit to Podere Sapaio is an excellent way to experience the region's modern winemaking philosophy, with a focus on sustainability and Bordeaux varietals. After a morning of tasting, Osteria Magona is a must for dining, offering Tuscan classics with a focus on local meats and Bolgheri wines – the bistecca is particularly well-regarded.

As a little detour or change of scenery, head to Castagneto Carducci, a nearby hilltop town offering breathtaking views over the vineyards and coastline. Named after the Nobel Prize-winning poet, this village provides a quieter, more traditional contrast to the sleek, wine-centric appeal of Bolgheri.

Viale dei Cipressi, Bolgheri

Wine routes

Chianti Classico; Montalcino to Pienzato; the hilltop towns of the south; Bolgheri, Maremma and the coastal towns – four wine routes to get the most out of your day in Tuscany. *Please refer to The Guide (see p128) for details of many of the wineries and other places mentioned.*

Cathedral of Santa Maria Assunta, Siena

Getting to Tuscany

Florence's international airport has connections from London, but no direct flights from anywhere in the US. There is also a low-cost route to Pisa from Bristol, Heathrow, Gatwick, Luton, Stansted and Manchester. A five-minute shuttle bus links the airport with the central station, and from here there are regular trains to Florence's Santa Maria Novella. The best way to explore Tuscany however is to hire a car, and while Florence is a natural draw, especially for those who haven't been, the real magic of Tuscany lies in its small towns and sprawling countryside. Each of these four itineraries suggests a mix of recommended wineries, great restaurants, cultural landmarks and places to stay.

Wine route 1
The Chianti Classico Villages

The best way to understand Chianti Classico is to drive through its hills, stopping not just in its famous villages but in the surrounding countryside. Spring and autumn are the most rewarding seasons, when the vineyards shift through shades of green and gold, and the roads are quiet enough to appreciate the scenery. The road south from Florence leads first to **Greve in Chianti**, historically a market hub for the surrounding estates. **Piazza Matteotti** is the village's focal point, lined with wine shops and enotecas stocking a wide range of Chianti Classico producers. Le Cantine di Greve is one of the most popular. The village hosts the annual **Chianti Classico Expo** every September.

A short detour to **Montefioralle,** considered one of the most beautiful villages in Italy, provides a glimpse of medieval Chianti, its fortifications once guarding key trade routes. Nearby, the **Vignamaggio** winery has an impressive library of older wines; an ideal place for lunch or dinner is **Castello di Gabbiano winery**'s restaurant, **Il Cavaliere**,

114

River Arno
67
Florence
Winery
Town/city
Railway station
River
Motorway
Main road/Minor road
Railway
RA3
Greve
in Chianti
Montefioralle
Vignamaggio
Panzano
Fontodi
Volpaia
Badia a
Coltibuono
429
Radda
Castellina
Gaiole
Castello La Leccia
Castello
di Ama
Castello di
Meleto
Castello
di Brolio
0
5 miles
0
5 kilometres
N

which is set within the vineyards and serves traditional Tuscan food.

From here, a short drive leads to **Panzano**, a village at the forefront of organic and sustainable viticulture in Chianti Classico. **Fontodi** stands out. Its flagship wine, Flaccianello, continues to be recognized as a top Tuscan wine, but the Gran Selezione 'Vigna del Sorbo' is increasingly considered a benchmark expression of Sangiovese. The village itself is small but lively, and home to the butcher **Cecchini**, where locally sourced beef is a speciality.

Leaving **Panzano**, the drive continues south to **Castellina**, where Chianti's history as a frontier territory is reflected in its well-preserved **15th-century fortress**. The village has a lively enoteca scene so it's good for a casual tasting, and it has a reputation for excellent cured meats. Nearby, **Castello di Ama** has a world-famous art collection and sculpture garden with pieces by artists such as Louise Bourgeois, Roni Horn and Anish Kapoor.

From Castellina, it's a short drive to **Radda**, known for its fresher style of Chianti Classico and its historic role as an administrative centre for the Chianti League (see p20) Nearby **Volpaia** is a medieval fortified hamlet; its vineyards are some of the highest in the region and produce wines with notable finesse and elegance.

The final stretch leads to **Gaiole**, once a key market hub and now the starting point for the **Strada dei Castelli**, a well-marked route linking historic wine estates. Among them are **Castello di Brolio**, the ancestral seat of the **Ricasoli** family; **Badia a Coltibuono**, a former monastery; and **Castello di Meleto**, a fortress surrounded by vineyards. Dine at **Il Ristoro di Ama** and try the signature wild boar ragù over fresh pappardelle.

If you're staying overnight, **Castello La Leccia** is a serene hilltop retreat with panoramic vineyard views, while **Borgo San Felice**, complete with a Michelin-starred restaurant, is more luxurious.

Wine route 2
Exploring Arezzo & Valdarno di Sopra

Tuscany's eastern hills, from **Arezzo** to Valdarno di Sopra, offer a quieter alternative to the more famous wine regions. The best way to explore them is by driving through their historic towns and rugged countryside, where vineyards rise from ancient terraces above the Arno River and Renaissance influences remain strong.

'Arezzo, with its fine Piazza Grande and the Church of San Francesco, has some of Tuscany's richest artistic and cinematic connections – and a thriving café and antique scene'

Your first stop (and a great base) should be **Il Borro**, a restored medieval hamlet that operates as a wine estate, boutique hotel and working farm. Purchased by Italian fashion dynasty the Ferragamo family in 1993, the estate has been transformed into a centre for organic viticulture, producing Sangiovese, Syrah and Chardonnay. As an aside, Massimo and Chiara Ferragamo were also behind Montalcino's extraordinary Castiglion del Bosco, before selling it to the Rosewood hotel group (see p146). At Il Borro you can tour the winery and vineyards and have a guided tasting, or pair the wines with locally sourced dishes at Osteria del Borro, the estate's restaurant, whose terrace looks over the weathered walls and pantiled roofs of the old houses of Il Borro. There's also a workshop where local artisans practise traditional leatherwork, goldsmithing and ceramics.

N
Winery
Town/city
Railway station
River
Motorway
Main road/Minor road
Railway
Regional boundary
Il Borro
Tenuta Sette Ponti
71
River Arno
Arezzo
A1
TUSCANY
Tenuta Licinia
Lucignano
Baracchi
Cortona
Fabrizio Dionisio
RA6
A1
Lago di Trasimeno
UMBRIA
Montepulciano
0
10 miles
0
10 kilometres

Nearby, **Tenuta Sette Ponti**, owned by the Moretti Cuseri family, takes its name from the historic Strada dei Sette Ponti, an ancient road crossing seven bridges between Florence and Arezzo, including the 12th-century Ponte Buriano, thought to be in the background of the Mona Lisa. Sette Ponti produces classy wines using both Sangiovese and Bordeaux varieties.

Arezzo is often overshadowed by Florence, but has some of Tuscany's richest artistic and cinematic connections. The medieval centre, with its fine Piazza Grande and the Church of San Francesco, home to Piero della Francesca's famous fresco cycle, was a location for Anthony Minghella's Oscar-laden 1996 film *The English Patient*, Roberto Benigni's *Life is Beautiful* (1997) and many others. Today, the town has a thriving café and antique scene. The Arno River, winding just north of the city, marks the transition from Arezzo's lively streets to the vineyards, olive groves and wooded slopes of Valdarno di Sopra DOC.

Continuing south-west, you come to the medieval hilltop village of **Lucignano**, on the northern edge of Valdichiana, whose elliptical street layout is unique in Tuscany. The nearby organic estate **Tenuta Licinia** produces high-altitude Sangiovese wines with impressive freshness. Winemaker James Marshall-Lockyer is focused on soil health, and a visit to the estate offers fascinating insight into vineyard terroir.

Cortona, which dates to Etruscan times, sits high above the Val di Chiana, with sweeping views towards Lake Trasimeno in Umbria. Amble up the steep streets to wide panoramic terraces, where cafés and wine bars have views across the valley. Cortona has a reputation for Syrah, with wineries like Fabrizio Dionisio and Baracchi producing elegant, spice-laden wines.

From here you can circle back into Tuscany's eastern hills and the chestnut forests of the foothills of the Apennines. The journey continues towards Arezzo's historic heart, back to your base across the Arno, or east into the lesser-explored wine regions that lie beyond.

Lucignano

Wine route 3
The hilltop towns of Southern Tuscany: Montalcino, Pienza, Montepulciano

Southern Tuscany is home to the historic hill towns of **Montalcino** and **Montepulciano**, whose identities have been shaped by wine over centuries. Montalcino, inescapably associated with its iconic wine, **Brunello**, now has hundreds of wineries to visit, high-quality restaurants and a range of wine-related accommodation. The town is small, and quiet for much of the day, but around **Piazza del Popolo**, cafés and wine bars see a steady flow of locals and visitors.

Biondi-Santi, the winery that pioneered Brunello, is an example of the traditional style, while **Casanova di Neri** has a modern interpretation, best experienced over lunch at its on-site restaurant. For accommodation, **Le Ragnaie** specializes in high-altitude Brunello, **Capanna Suites** is a vineyard retreat, and **Castiglion del Bosco** is a luxury resort with its own winery and golf course, created out of a deserted feudal town with ruined 12-century castle, twenty farms, a police station and the 14th-century chapel of San Michele Arcangelo, with its 1345 mural by Pietro Lorenzetti. **Castello Banfi**, one of the largest estates in the area, produces structured, internationally recognized wines in a setting that blends medieval architecture with modern winemaking.

From Montalcino, take the road east through the **Val d'Orcia**, a rural area with open farmland, small villages and scattered olive groves. Stop at **Pienza** to see its compact historic centre designed during the Renaissance as an ideal town, and have a simple lunch of local bread, cured meats and aged **Pecorino**, a speciality of Pienza and sold everywhere. The town's elevated position

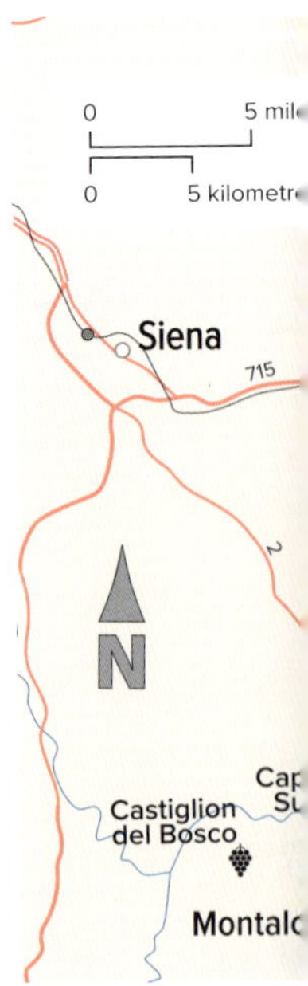

provides views across the Val d'Orcia's famed hills, with Montepulciano visible in the distance.

A short drive from Pienza, **Montepulciano** is a larger hill town, known for **Vino Nobile di Montepulciano** (see p68). The streets are lined with Renaissance palaces, and the **Piazza Grande** is the centre of local life. Many wineries here have underground cellars carved into the stone beneath the buildings.

At **Avignonesi**, you can explore biodynamic vineyards and taste different expressions of Vino Nobile, with lunch available overlooking the vines. **Salcheto winery** offers tastings and modern Tuscan food at its **Indigeno** restaurant. Just outside town, the 16th century Renaissance church **Tempio di San Biagio** is worth a visit.

From Montepulciano, the road continues towards Arezzo, where the vineyards give way to forested hills.

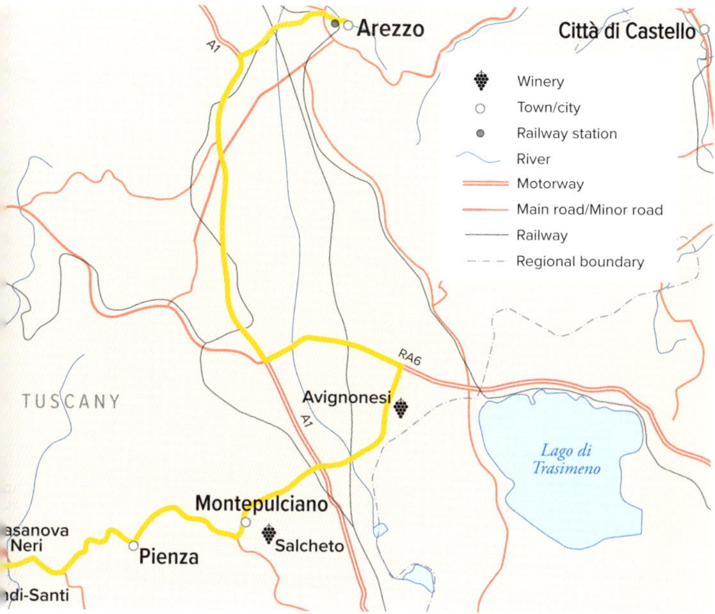

N
1
A12
Volterra
Caiarossa
Tenuta
San Guido
Bolgheri
Ornellaia
Grattamacco
Tenuta
Sette Cieli
TUSCANY
Tenuta
Argentiera
Tua Rita
Ampeleia
Morisfarms
Piombino
1
Isola
d'Elba
0
10 miles
0
10 kilometres
Castiglione
della Pescaia

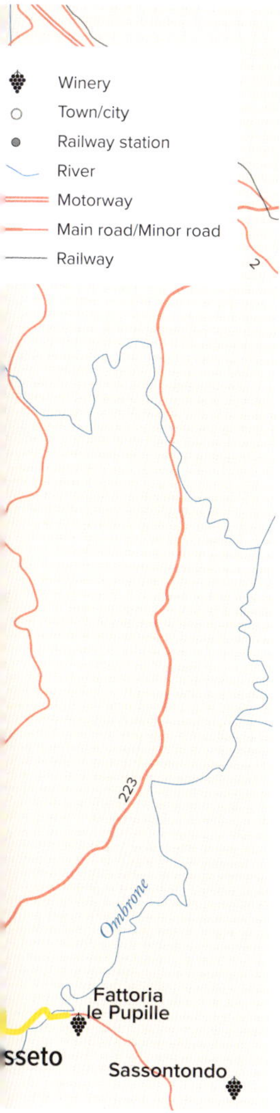

Wine route 4 Bolgheri, Maremma & the Tuscan Coast

A visit to **Bolgheri** and **Maremma** is a chance to explore Tuscany's coastal wine regions – home of the Super-Tuscans (see p35), where Bordeaux-inspired blends and native varieties thrive in very different conditions from the Sangiovese-dominated heartland of Chianti and Montalcino. Exploring Maremma is a compelling wine experience, giving you an insight into Tuscany's diverse terroir, where international varieties and local grapes coexist.

The **Viale dei Cipressi**, a gorgeous avenue of towering cypress trees, leads into the village of Bolgheri. The historic centre is filled with wine shops and restaurants that offer some of the best opportunities to taste the region's famous Super-Tuscan wines. Places like **Enoteca Tognoni** and **Enoteca di Bolgheri** allow visitors to compare wines from estates such as **Sassicaia**, **Ornellaia** and **Guado al Tasso**, alongside smaller producers. Restaurants **Osteria Magona** and **La Pineta** provide pairings that highlight the structure and depth of these wines, which differ from traditional Tuscan reds due to their use of Cabernet Sauvignon, Merlot and Syrah.

A visit to **Tenuta San Guido,** home to Sassicaia, provides a deeper understanding of how this Bordeaux-style blend became Italy's first officially recognized Super-Tuscan. Tastings at **Ornellaia** and **Grattamacco** show the range of styles in Bolgheri. **Tenuta Argentiera**, with its high-altitude vineyards overlooking the coast, produces some of the most refined expressions of Cabernet Sauvignon in the region, while **Tenuta Sette Cieli**, in the hills above Bolgheri, focuses on elegant, high-altitude blends. Nearby, biodynamic Caiarossa experiments with a mix of international and native varieties, producing wines with strong mineral and herbal character.

'Tua Rita's Merlot-driven wines helped put Maremma on the map'

From Bolgheri, the drive south follows the **Etruscan Coast**, passing through olive groves and wild Mediterranean vegetation towards **Maremma**, a region historically known for cattle farming and now home to some of Tuscany's most exciting modern wineries. Stop at **Tua Rita**, in the hills near Suvereto, to try Merlot-driven wines, particularly **Redigaffi**, which helped put Maremma on the map as a region of opulent, internationally acclaimed reds. Further inland, Maremma's winemaking identity shifts towards Ciliegiolo, a lesser-known but increasingly celebrated grape variety (see p45). Estates such as **Morisfarms**, **Antonio Camillo** and **Sassotondo** make vibrant, fruit-forward Ciliegiolo with floral aromas and bright acidity – a contrast to the dense, structured reds of Bolgheri**. Fattoria Le Pupille**, one of the region's most respected estates, produces both a benchmark Morellino di Scansano and the highly regarded Saffredi, a blend that rivals Bolgheri's best Super-Tuscans. If you have time, go to Castiglione della Pescaia for its hilltop views, pristine beaches and charming harbour. Further north, **Ampeleia**, set in the rugged inland hills, takes a different approach, focusing on Grenache, Carignan and Alicante Bouschet.

Castiglione della Pescaia

Tenuta San Guido: the medieval fortress of Castiglioncello di Bolgheri overlooks the Sassicaia vineyards.

LISTINGS PREPARED BY

Paul Caputo
Rebecca Ann Hughes
Phoebe Hunt
Emily O'Hare

The Guide

Contents

The best wineries for tours and tastings

There has never been a better time to travel through Tuscany. Over the years, wineries have become more and more hospitable: if you want to visit and taste, your options include medieval castles, aristocratic villas, modern commercial wineries, rustic agricultural estates and the charming farmsteads of independent winemakers. Plenty of these estates also have hotels, restaurants and wine bars. There are thousands of wineries in Tuscany, most of which welcome visitors, so narrowing down the best is no small task. Here is a curated list of some of the most worthwhile stops.

Tenuta Argentiera

PISA

Fattoria Fibbiano

Via Fibbiano, 2 - 56030 - Terricciola (Pisa)

Nicola Cantoni and his brother run a very casual *agriturismo* and tasting room, where you can sample some coastal wines with a distinctive maritime influence. The vineyards are full of white shells and marine deposits, imparting a sense of place and a reminder of the land's past life under water. From here, you can see and smell the sea. The Ciliegiolo is delicious, as is the very quaffable white from a rare grape variety – Colombana.

fattoria-fibbiano.it

Fattoria Fibbiano

SAN GIMIGNANO

Mormoraia

Loc. Sant'Andrea - 53037 - San Gimignano (SI)

Located just outside the medieval town of San Gimignano, Mormoraia produces some of the most distinctive expressions of Vernaccia you can find. A patchwork of vineyards and olive groves hug the hillsides and separate the winery, a former convent, from the famous 13th-century stone towers across the valley. Certified organic, the wines benefit from a gentle touch of oak and can be enjoyed as part of a guided tour of the property and cellar at this tranquil *agriturismo*.

mormoraia.it

CHIANTI RUFINA

Castello del Trebbio

Via Santa Brigida, 9 - 50065 - Pontassieve (Florence)

Castello del Trebbio was at the heart of the rivalry between Florence and Siena, and a visit brings some of this influential history to life. The medieval halls, atmospheric cellars and sprawling castle grounds enrich this window into a very different style of Chianti. Here the cooler 'Rufina' hills give a fresh, almost rustic personality to the wines. If you're calling in early, the estate's traditional-method sparkling is a good start.

castellodeltrebbio.com

Where winemakers dine

The best restaurant in Chianti Classico is **Enoteca Baldi** in Panzano. It is perfect in all aspects. They have an amazing wine list and presentation, well-trained staff and a fantastic head sommelier in the person of Gianmaria. All of this I consider to be fundamental to its success. A lot of research and passion goes into the artisanal, authentic and simple food, completing the picture of one of the best, if not *the* best, restaurant-enotecas in the area. For me, it's easily my favourite.

Alessandro Campatelli, Riecine, Chianti Classico

CHIANTI CLASSICO

Castello di Gabbiano

Via di Gabbiano, 22 - 50024 - Mercatale Val di Pesa (Firenze)

At Castello di Gabbiano, history and wine converge. The earliest records date to the 11th century, when a square tower was built to defend a key route between Florence and Siena. Today, the fortified castle and vaulted cellars make this a pleasant stop. Wander the estate's 147 hectares, where vineyards snake through clay-limestone soils. In the winery's restaurant, Il Cavaliere, traditional Tuscan cuisine is served alongside Bellezza, the flagship Chianti Classico Gran Selezione. Delicious Vin Santo from Trebbiano and Malvasia are available to toast a great lunch.

castellogabbiano.it

Badia a Coltibuono

Loc. Badia a Coltibuono, Gaiole in Chianti - 53013 (SI)

Set in a captivating monastic setting dating back to 1051, this legendary estate just outside Gaiole cultivates primarily Sangiovese for its highly regarded Chianti Classico. Managed by the fifth generation of the Stucchi Prinetti family, the expansive 700-hectare property features 70 hectares under vine and invests heavily in organic viticulture. The estate also offers an authentic *agriturismo* and restaurant – ideal for weddings, personalized tastings and cooking classes. Don't miss the homemade *schiacciata*, a flatbread similar to focaccia.

coltibuono.com

Querceto di Castellina

Loc. Querceto, 9 - 53011 - Castellina in Chianti (SI)

Located in the hills at 500 metres, between Radda and Castellina in Chianti, this family-run vineyard and boutique *agriturismo* offers a cool-climate expression of Chianti Classico. The Di Battista family crafts exceptional wines, including a unique white Viognier found nowhere else, and invites you to enjoy a home-cooked lunch, relax through the afternoon or watch the sunset behind the surrounding forests.

quercetodicastellina.com

Riecine

Località Riecine, 28/b - 53013 - Gaiole in Chianti (SI)

Riecine's wines are marked by a cool freshness – and one visit to the vineyards helps explain why. Located in the most northern part of Gaiole in Chianti, where altitudes get as high as 500m, these are some of Chianti Classico's lightest and most vibrant wines. Alessandro Campatelli is making the wines now, and continues Riecine's legacy as a Sangiovese specialist. Cement vats have been artistically decorated, depicting contemporary vineyard scenes. An informal tasting space gives a rustic vibe, but these are premium wines. Surrounded by biodynamic vineyards and life that buzzes around them, this is the place to be on a sunny spring morning.

riecine.it

Riecine

LUCIGNANO

Tenuta Licinia

Tenuta Licinia, Località Meleto il Calcione, Lucignano (AR) - 52046

If you want an education in the impact of subsoils on your wine, call in at Tenuta Licinia on your way to the medieval town of Lucignano. The wines are stunning, especially the Bordeaux blend 'Sasso di Fata', and winemaker James Marshall-Lockyer will set the scene with real insight into what terroir means in this part of Tuscany. His passion is infectious, and you'll feel like you're on a viticultural journey with him. Following a visit, don't be surprised to find yourself looking up the weather in Lucignano as the harvest approaches.

tenutalicinia.com

AREZZO

Tenuta Sette Ponti

Via Sette Ponti 71 - 52029 - Castiglion Fibocchi (AR)

Named after the Seven Bridges over the River Arno – one of which is thought to appear in the background of the Mona Lisa – Tenuta Sette Ponti ranks among the best wine visits in eastern Tuscany. Just outside Arezzo, entrepreneur Antonio Moretti has built a sanctuary for outstanding wines, including selections from sister properties in Bolgheri and Sicily. Guests can enjoy tastings that celebrate the estate's old-vine heritage, scenic vineyard walks and authentic, locally sourced cuisine.

tenutasetteponti.it

Tenuta Sette Ponti

MONTALCINO

Fattoria dei Barbi

Società Agricola Località Podernovi, 170 Strada Consorziale dei Barbi - 53024 - Montalcino (SI)

Barbi is one of the great historic names of Montalcino and is worth a visit for its museum alone. Hospitality is central to the company, though, and a range of structured tours and tastings are available, including a stop at the dairy farm where visitors can enjoy produce from Montalcino's oldest cheese-making facilities. This centuries-old tradition focuses exclusively on sheep's milk.

fattoriadeibarbi.it

Le Ragnaie

Loc. Le Ragnaie - 53024 - Montalcino (SI)

Le Ragnaie near Montalcino has growing cult status and serious wine lovers should have the estate on their radar. Not only are the wines exceptional, they're also very affordable. With some of the highest vineyards in the DOCG, the style is cool and fresh. In fact, the vines are so high, the area was used by bird catchers, hence the big net on the labels. Visits are by appointment – but it's well worth reaching out before the secret is truly out.

leragnaie.com

Poggio Antico

Loc. Poggio Antico - 53024 - Montalcino SI, Italy

Poggio Antico has some of the highest vineyards in Montalcino, situated right in the heart of the appellation. There's always a cooling breeze here and on a clear day the views stretch for miles. The wines are some of the freshest Brunello you can find. Great for a quick educational stop on your way in or out of town.

poggioantico.com

BOLGHERI

Ornellaia

Località Ornellaia, 191, Fraz. Bolgheri, 57022 Castagneto Carducci

Established in 1981, this prestigious Italian estate, owned by the Frescobaldi family, is renowned for its Cabernet-dominated Super-Tuscan wines. A guided tour takes you through historic vineyards and a cellar showcasing the Vendemmia d'Artista project, where contemporary artworks celebrate each vintage. Enjoy a scenic picnic beneath an ancient oak with stunning Bolgheri views, or explore the evolution of this legendary wine through an in-depth look at the history of the Ornellaia, accompanied by an immersive vertical tasting that includes important back vintages.

ornellaia.com

Tenuta Argentiera

Via Aurelia 410 - 57022 - Castagneto Carducci (LI), frazione di Donoratico

Set in the Bolgheri DOC, Tenuta Argentiera offers an immersive wine tour that highlights its coastal vineyards, distinctive terroir and Bordeaux-inspired blends. Guests can explore the state-of-the-art winery, learn about the estate's commitment to elevation-driven viticulture and enjoy guided tastings of its acclaimed Argentiera, Villa Donoratico and Poggio

Tenuta Argentiera

ai Ginepri wines. A visit to Argentiera provides a deep dive into one of Bolgheri's most important wine estates, and also offers sweeping views of the Tyrrhenian Sea.

argentiera.eu

Grattamacco

Loc. Lungagnano 128 - 57022 - Castagneto Carducci (LI)

As the second estate established in Bolgheri, Grattamacco is a true pioneer of the region. Its wines remain outstanding, and tours offer a behind-the-scenes look at their process. This is a chance to stand in their legendary vineyards and contemplate the characteristics of terroir. More than just a visit, tastings include library vintages, showcasing the evolution of one of Tuscany's great wines.

grattamacco.it

MAREMMA

Ampeleia

Località Meleta - 58036 - Roccatederighi (GR), Maremma

Ampeleia is a winemaking project set in the wild hills and forests of the Maremma. At 500m, cooling breezes help to make very fresh Cabernet Franc and Sangiovese. If this feels off the beaten path, it's because it is. Founded in 2002, this

Where winemakers dine

My favourite restaurant is **Il Doretto** in Cecina. They have a fantastic wine list, ranging from exquisite Champagne to legendary Italian and international wines. The food is exceptional, with top-quality dishes for both seafood and meat lovers. The atmosphere resembles the living room of a beautiful villa. It's informal and cosy, the perfect place for an unforgettable dining experience.

Nicolò Carrara, Argentiera, Bolgheri

30-hectare estate converted to biodynamic farming in 2009 and the wines are bottled without fining or filtration, with minimal sulphur and oak. Enjoy tastings in its agriturismo restaurant, and move on for lunch or dinner in the charming nearby village of Roccatederighi.

ampeleia.it

Castello di Vicarello

Loc Vicarello 1, Poggi del Sasso Cinigiano (GR) - 58044

There is something of the fairytale castle about Castello di Vicarello, making it easy to see why two Milanese fashionistas would want to escape the city and put their mark on it. You can see for miles across the wild, forested hills of the Maremma. Perhaps there is no better view in Tuscany, especially as the golden hour descends (and it's worth noting you can stay at its hotel overnight). Wine tastings include the region's speciality rosé, made from Sangiovese, Cabernet and Merlot. For better or worse, no children under 10.

castellodivicarello.com

MONTEPULCIANO

Boscarelli

Via di Montenero, 24 - 53045 - Montepulciano, Italy

Boscarelli, the star name of Montepulciano winemaking, is nestled in Cervognano, east of the town towards Valdichiana. Founded in 1962 by Egidio Corradi and now managed by the third generation, this 22-hectare organic estate produces around 100,000 bottles each year – most of which is Vino Nobile. Vineyard tours, tastings and cellar visits are all possible (paired with the quintessential local lunch of pici in wild boar ragù) and showcase how Sangiovese harmonizes with southern Tuscany's varied soils.

poderiboscarelli.com

Winery hotels

Many Tuscan estates now offer overnight stays, allowing you to immerse yourself in the landscape, tradition and wine of the region. Whether medieval castle, restored hamlet (or *borgo*) or contemporary vineyard retreat, these wine hotels offer more than just accommodation – they provide a gateway to Tuscany's winemaking heritage.

San Felice panoramica ufficiale

Borgo San Felice, a beautifully restored medieval village in Chianti Classico, combines Relais & Châteaux luxury with access to some of the region's most expressive Sangiovese wines. Castello Banfi, set within a historic fortress near Montalcino, offers vertical tastings of Brunello and Tuscan-inspired dining at La Sala dei Grappoli. At Castello La Leccia, in the Chianti hills, you can enjoy organic Sangiovese and an infinity pool overlooking the vines. In Gaiole in Chianti, Capannelle Wine Resort has just five rooms... The following is a selection of the best wine-immersive stays.

CHIANTI RUFINA

Castello di Nipozzano

Castello Nipozzano, Frescobaldi, Località Nipozzano - 50060 - Nipozzano (FI)

A fortified stronghold since the year 1,000, Castello di Nipozzano is the most historic estate of the Frescobaldi family, a dynasty that has shaped Tuscan winemaking for centuries. Overlooking the rugged Chianti Rufina hills, the castle's ancient stone walls and grand halls are atmospheric, while the boutique hotel and spa are fittingly upmarket. The vineyards, planted in 1855, introduced Cabernet Sauvignon, Merlot, Cabernet Franc and Petit Verdot to Tuscany, forming the foundation of Mormoreto, the estate's iconic wine. Guests can enjoy exclusive tastings, cellar tours and gourmet dining surrounded by history, where Renaissance artists like Donatello once sourced their wine. A true immersion in Tuscany's noble winemaking tradition.

frescobaldi.com/it/tenute/castello-nipozzano

CHIANTI COLLI FIOREN-TINI

Casa Ruffino

P.Le Ruffino, 1 - 50065 - Pontassieve (FI)

Casa Ruffino, nestled within the Tenuta Ruffino Poggio Casciano estate near Florence, less than 10 miles from Ponte Vecchio, is an intimate address with eight double rooms, each uniquely furnished and equipped to a high standard. Guests can unwind by the infinity pool, which overlooks the verdant Tuscan hills. Breakfast gives a taste of the good life, with dishes served on the terrace overlooking serene country views. The estate's gourmet Tre

Casa Ruffino

Rane Restaurant serves elevated traditional Tuscan cuisine à la carte and in a setting that features white tablecloths under chandeliers, with a selection of Ruffino's top wines served in elegant stemware. Explore the winery through immersive tours and tastings, delving into a history that dates back to 1877. The Enoteca Ruffino stocks the entire portfolio, including old vintages and limited-edition releases.

ruffino.it/pages/casa-ruffino

CHIANTI CLASSICO

San Felice

Località San Felice - 53019 - Castelnuovo Berardenga (Siena)

Borgo San Felice, a medieval hamlet turned luxury retreat in Chianti Classico, offers elegant Relais & Châteaux accommodation amidst a working vineyard. Renowned for its 'Il Grigio' wines, and more recently its Michelin-starred restaurant, Poggio Rosso, the estate blends history with a contemporary international feel. Guests can enjoy sweeping views over the vines, fine dining and a wine list inclusive of sister property labels in Montalcino and Bolgheri. A fabulous destination for those seeking upscale hospitality alongside rustic Tuscan charm; perfect for couples and larger groups.

borgosanfelice.com

Castello di Meleto

Castello di Meleto - 53013 - Gaiole in Chianti (SI)

Castello di Meleto is a storybook retreat in the heart of Chianti, offering a true taste of life on a working wine estate – and surrounded by some of Chianti's most renowned wineries, just an hour from Florence, 45 minutes from Siena and a short drive from Gaiole in Chianti. With accommodation ranging from castle rooms to nearby farmhouses, it's ideal for both families on longer stays and couples seeking a

Castello di Meleto

short countryside escape. The estate's wines can be enjoyed in the enoteca, where a light lunch menu features local specialities, including estate-reared *cinta senese* pork. Steeped in history, the castle dates back to the 11th century and was once a summer residence of the Ricasoli family. Today, it remains a charming retreat right in the thick of Chianti country.

castellomeleto.it

Monteverdi Tuscany

Via di Mezzo, Castiglioncello del Trinoro - 53047 - Sarteano (SI)

Nestled in the rolling hills of Castiglioncello del Trinoro, Monteverdi Tuscany is a secluded luxury retreat that blends art, design and world-class wine experiences. More than just a hotel, it is an immersive cultural destination, offering beautifully restored stone villas and suites with breathtaking views over the Val d'Orcia. The estate's vineyards, planted with Sangiovese, Cabernet Franc and Merlot, produce small quantities of wines that reflect the region's terroir. Guests can enjoy exclusive tastings, private vineyard tours and food at Oreade, the hotel's fine-dining restaurant. The Monteverdi Culinary Academy

Where winemakers dine

I am very happy to recommend **Il Leccio**, a family-run restaurant located in the charming square of Sant'Angelo in Colle. It looks out over the surrounding panorama in all directions – from the dense oak woods and Mediterranean scrub that rise up towards Montalcino, to the mighty and wild Monte Amiata. The Tognazzi family ran one of the most prestigious restaurants in the country for over two decades, and then dedicated themselves to simple and genuine cuisine, strongly linked to local tradition. With great attention to seasonality and local products, Il Leccio offers dishes in which pici, bread soup, wild boar, handmade pasta, roasts, cheeses and *scottiglia* [a typical Tuscan stew] are the real protagonists: rich in history and authenticity, without artifice, ready to tell their story to those who know how to appreciate it.

Leopoldo Franceschi,
La Casaccia di Franceschi,
Montalcino

offers immersive food and wine experiences, while the on-site spa provides holistic treatments inspired by Tuscany's natural elements. With its refined atmosphere and commitment to artisanal luxury, Monteverdi Tuscany is a destination for discerning travellers seeking elegance, culture and a deep connection to wine and place.

monteverdituscany.com

Castello La Leccia

Loc. La Leccia - 53011 - Castellina in Chianti (SI)

Set in the hills above Castellina in Chianti, Castello La Leccia offers sweeping views across vineyards and olive groves towards San Gimignano, Monteriggioni and Siena. The restored medieval castle provides history and atmosphere, while its 12 contemporary rooms have a unique personality. Breakfast is served in the Limonaia, a conservatory filled with lemon trees, or outdoors, where guests can take in the landscape while enjoying homemade cakes, fresh cheeses and Tuscan bread. Lunch is a relaxed affair, best enjoyed by the pool or under ancient holm oaks with a glass of wine, and as the sun sets, an aperitivo in the gardens sets the tone for an evening at the estate's zero-kilometre restaurant. Castello La Leccia is a place to lose yourself in the rhythms of Tuscan country life.

castellolaleccia.com

Capannelle Wine Resort

Località Capannelle, 13 - 53013 - Gaiole in Chianti (Siena)

The Capannelle Wine Resort is a family-friendly retreat set within a historic 16th-century villa in the heart of Chianti Classico. The boutique accommodations offer just five luxurious rooms, blending the rusticity of a renovated stone farmhouse with modern comforts. Guests can enjoy private cellar tours, tastings of Capannelle's acclaimed Chianti Classico and

Il Borro

50&50 Super-Tuscan, and tailor-made wine experiences for larger groups. The panoramic infinity pool, set among the vines, enhances the tranquil atmosphere. Located in Gaiole in Chianti, it's also conveniently close to other key attractions, making this a very practical base from which to explore.

capannelle.it/wineresort/resort/

AREZZO

Il Borro

Location Il Borro 1 - 52024 - San Giustino v.no Arezzo

Il Borro, a restored medieval hamlet and wine estate owned by the Ferragamo family, spans 1,100 hectares of vineyards, olive groves and organic farmland. Certified organic since 2015, the Il Borro winery produces terroir-driven wines, including the highly scored Il Borro Toscana IGT, a Merlot, Cabernet Sauvignon and Syrah blend, alongside expressive Sangiovese-based wines. Guests can explore these through private tastings and cellar tours. Accommodations range from luxurious villas to suites within the medieval village, blending historic charm with modern comfort. Osteria del Borro showcases estate-grown ingredients in refined Tuscan dishes, while a spa, artisan workshops and equestrian centre may make it hard to find reason to ever leave the premises. Rooted in tradition and sustainability, Il Borro is an impressive retreat and one of the most important wine estates in the east of Tuscany.

ilborro.it

CORTONA

Relais Falconiere & Spa

Loc. San Martino a Bocena, 370 - 52044 - Cortona (AR)

Cypresses, umbrella pines, silver-green olive trees and vineyards as far as the eye can see. What more can you want? Just outside the medieval town of Cortona, this modern spa facility by Relais & Châteaux is both a peaceful retreat and boutique family-run wine estate. Once a 17th-century noble villa, the property houses a Michelin-starred restaurant, overseen by the Baracchi family, who have deep ties to Tuscan winemaking. The Sereno Spa, set within a converted lemon house, offers wine therapy treatments in the pursuit of holistic well-being. They can include an antioxidant bath with red wine extracts, thought to stimulate circulation and smooth the skin, as well as a regenerating massage. The Baracchi Winery, known for its expressive Syrah and Sangiovese wines, invites guests to enjoy cellar tours and guided tastings. With panoramic views, antique-filled interiors and farm-to-table dining, Il Falconiere is all about understated Tuscan luxury.

ilfalconiere.it

MONTALCINO

Capanna Suites

Località Valdicava - 53024 (Siena)

Just down the road from the Capanna winery, Capanna Suites offers an intimate retreat on the edge of Montalcino. An on-site pool, restaurant and wellness facilities support a choice of well-finished apartments. The elegantly restored suites combine traditional warmth with a touch of understated luxury, while the spa offers various treatments infused with local ingredients. From the terrace, guests can take in the soft morning mist drifting over the vineyards, before enjoying a leisurely breakfast in full view of idyllic valley slopes. The same uninterrupted view stretches from the infinity pool, a perfect spot to unwind with a glass of the estate's Rosso di Montalcino. Dining is classic, refined Tuscan cuisine supported by a library of back Brunello vintages, allowing guests to explore the evolution of Capanna's wines over decades.

capannasuites.com

Castello Banfi

Castello di Poggio alle Mura - 53024 - Montalcino, Siena

Set within the historic Castello Banfi, Il Borgo provides an immersive stay at one of Montalcino's most recognized wine estates. The hotel balances medieval character with modern comfort, offering suites that overlook the vineyards and olive groves. Breakfast on

Capanna Suites

Where winemakers dine

If you want to find authentic Tuscan cuisine in a place steeped in history, **Buca di San Francesco** is the perfect spot. Located in the heart of Arezzo, this restaurant welcomes guests into a medieval cellar with vaulted ceilings and stone walls, creating an intimate and authentic atmosphere. The menu celebrates tradition with dishes like ribollita and *pappa ai carciofi*. It's a timeless place where the service is warm yet impeccable, and every dish tells the story of the region. Perfect for a relaxed dinner, perhaps after a day among the vineyards.

Amadeo Moretti Cuseri, Tenuta Sette Ponti, Arezzo

the terrace sets the tone for a day spent exploring the Banfi winery, where guests can taste the estate's 'Poggio alle Mura' Brunello. Exclusive tastings highlight the estate's flagship wines, while La Taverna restaurant pairs them with all the usual seasonal dishes. The Banfi Wine & Glass Museum adds further depth, tracing the evolution of the estate's winemaking and glassmaking traditions. In Montalcino terms, Banfi is a prominent corporate player, but in combining fine wines, hospitality and heritage, Castello Banfi–Il Borgo has become a familiar reference point for the area and will appeal to both enthusiasts and those starting out on their wine journey.

banfi.it

Castiglion del Bosco

Rosewood Castiglion del Bosco, Località Castiglion del Bosco - 53024 - Montalcino (Siena)

Castiglion del Bosco offers a secluded retreat, set as it is within a 5,000-acre private estate, where luxury hospitality meets a deep-rooted winemaking tradition. Founded by Massimo and Chiara Ferragamo, this Rosewood resort is built around a carefully restored 900-year-old borgo.

Castiglion del Bosco

Suites and villas feature terracotta tones, exposed beams and handcrafted furnishings, balancing historic character with understated comfort. Private terraces overlook the vineyards, reinforcing the estate's tranquil and exclusive atmosphere. Guests can explore Castiglion del Bosco's Brunello di Montalcino through guided tastings, participate in the harvest or dine at Osteria La Canonica, where Tuscan ingredients and dishes inevitably dominate. This is one of the most exclusive destinations in Tuscany, and undoubtedly, with prices to match, at the top end of wine hospitality.

rosewoodhotels.com/castiglion-del-bosco

Conti di San Bonifacio

Società Agricola Poggio Divino srl, Località Casteani 1 - 58023 - Gavorrano (GR)

Nestled in the hills of Maremma, Conti di San Bonifacio is a boutique wine resort that blends rustic elegance, organic winemaking and simple but authentic Tuscan hospitality. Created by Count Manfredo and Countess Sarah di San Bonifacio, the estate is a labour of love, with seven hectares of meticulously tended vineyards producing award-winning wines under the expertise of consulting winemaker Luca d'Attoma. The Maremmana Restaurant, perched serenely on the hilltop, embraces a farm-to-table ethos, using organic ingredients from the estate's own garden. The interiors balance local craftsmanship with designer touches, while a pool with panoramic views and the Tree Lounge Bar create a chilled-out, social atmosphere. Guests can immerse themselves in vineyard life, from wine tastings to harvest experiences, making this a true wine lover's escape.

contidisanbonifacio.com
capannelle.it

Winery restaurants

Many of Tuscany's wineries offer guests the opportunity to pair their wines with local cuisine, but some have taken this further, establishing full-scale restaurants that have become integral to the region's food and wine culture. Eating out in Italy is often about conviviality – simple dishes, good company and well-chosen wine. Trattorias, osterias and pizzerias dominate the landscape, but winery restaurants add another dimension.

Rinuccio 1180

Many of the region's finest winery restaurants are set in historic estates with deep-rooted traditions, some dating back to the Renaissance and beyond. Once seen as overly formal or old-fashioned, these grand dining halls – adorned with family portraits and noble insignia – are now at the forefront of the growing demand for authenticity. With direct access to estate-grown ingredients and an inherent sense of place, they are uniquely positioned to offer immersive, farm-to-table experiences that blend storytelling with exceptional hospitality.

When a winery creates a restaurant, the menu is never an afterthought. Every dish is designed to enhance the wines, forging a deeper connection between the glass and the plate. While a tasting room visit offers insight, there's no better way to experience a wine's true character than by sharing a bottle at the table, surrounded by food that speaks the same language.

CARMIGNANO

Vinsantaia (Capezzana)

Via Capezzana, 100 - 59015 - Carmignano Prato

Vinsantaia is a restaurant deeply connected to the region's winemaking traditions. Housed, as you might deduce, in a former *Vinsantaia*, where Vin Santo barrels once aged, the space retains a rustic elegance, with exposed beams and soft lighting creating a warm atmosphere. The menu highlights Tuscan flavours in a contemporary style, featuring fresh pasta, local meats and estate-grown produce. The restaurant is part of the historic Capezzana estate in Carmignano DOCG, which means the wine list focuses on the local wines, particularly the historic Sangiovese-Cabernet blends that define the appellation. Back vintages of Vin Santo, Capezzana's flagship sweet wine, are also available and are highly recommended. Many of the ingredients are sourced fresh from the property's organic farm. Thoughtful cooking and historic surroundings make this one of the most important dining spots in Carmignano.

lavinsantaia.it

CHIANTI CLASSICO

Poggio Rosso (San Felice)

150 Località San Felice - 53019 - Castelnuovo Berardenga (Siena)

Not every fine-dining restaurant in Tuscany has to be a traditional Tuscan experience. At Poggio Rosso, the kitchen embraces an international perspective, crafting dishes that draw on global influences while still incorporating ingredients from the estate, such as fresh herbs from its garden. This approach has earned the restaurant a Michelin star, recognizing its ability to balance innovation with local identity. Set within the Borgo San Felice estate, the dining space blends historic charm with contemporary elegance. Chianti Classico and Super-Tuscan wines feature heavily on the list, alongside selections from sister wineries in Bolgheri and Montalcino. Poggio Rosso offers a modern fine-dining experience in the heart of Tuscany, and when combined with a stay at the San Felice hotel, makes for a luxurious time in Siena's Castelnuovo Berardenga.

borgosanfelice.com

Where winemakers dine

Osteria del Borgo offers an authentic Tuscan experience in the heart of Montepulciano. It's in a splendid 14th-century palace in the beautiful Piazza Grande. This warm and inviting family-run restaurant has a menu that stays true to Tuscan tradition, with handmade pasta and locally sourced ingredients. The wine list features selections from all across Europe, but of course there is a focus on Tuscan wines. We love to sit on the terrace, looking out over the Tuscan countryside and drinking a glass of Vino Nobile.

Paolo Caciorgna, Cantine Dei, Montepulciano

Il Cavaliere (Castello di Gabbiano)

Via di Gabbiano 12 - 50026 - Mercatale V.P.

Alfresco dining is symbolic of the good life, and the outdoor lunches at Il Cavaliere are as evocative as the postcards. Il Cavaliere is an extension of the Castello di Gabbiano estate and is set in a carefully restored 16th-century farmhouse surrounded by vineyards. The interiors feature stone walls and frescoed ceilings, while the outdoor terrace provides a peaceful setting overlooking the estate. The menu follows the rhythm of the seasons, using fresh ingredients from local producers with a focus on classic Tuscan recipes. Dishes include handmade pasta, risottos and the usual Florentine specialities. The pigeon, when it's on the menu, comes highly recommended. The wine list highlights Castello di Gabbiano's range of Chianti Classico, along with other top wines from the region and beyond. The combination of historical atmosphere and considered cooking makes Il Cavaliere a distinctive part of Gabbiano's winemaking heritage and this is a much-loved reference on Chianti's dining scene.

ilcavalieredigabbiano.it

Il Ristoro di Ama (Castello di Ama)

Castello di Ama, Località Ama - 53013 - Gaiole in Chianti (Siena)

Il Ristoro di Ama, the fine-dining restaurant of Castello di Ama in Chianti Classico, offers an elegant yet relaxed experience deeply rooted in the estate's traditions. Housed in a historic stone building, it serves a seasonal, ingredient-driven menu designed to pair seamlessly with the estate's Chianti Classico and single-vineyard Gran Selezione wines. The signature wild boar ragù over fresh pappardelle is a must-try, capturing the magical simplicity of Tuscan cuisine. Guests can dine on the terrace overlooking the vineyards, or indoors surrounded by contemporary art from the estate's collection. For an even more immersive experience, the 'Feast of Villa Pianigiani' offers a special culinary celebration, bringing together an indulgent mix of the estate's wine and food traditions. Part of the fabric of the local fine-dining scene, and easily one of Tuscany's best wine-focused restaurants.

castellodiama.com/en/ristoro

Rinuccio 1180 (Antinori)

Via Cassia per Siena, 133
Loc. Bargino - 50026 - San Casciano val di Pesa, Firenze

Antinori has developed a stylish rooftop terrace located within the flagship Chianti Classico winery, where impressive contemporary architecture blends with the landscape. Named after Rinuccio di Antinori, who in 1180 was the first-recorded Antinori family member to make wine, the restaurant sits atop the winery, offering sweeping views of the vines. The menu draws inspiration from Tuscan tradition, using high-quality local ingredients, while incorporating a modern approach to presentation and technique. The Florentine T-bone with roasted potatoes is highly recommended and goes with most reds on the wine list. The sleek, open-dining space reflects the winery's avant-garde aesthetic, while the outdoor terrace provides a direct view of the land. It acts as a natural extension of the Antinori brand, providing a hospitality space to combine both heritage and innovation.

antinori.it

Novecento (Dievole)

Wine Resort, Località Dievole 6 - 53019 - Castelnuovo Berardenga SI

Novecento takes its name from the Dievole winery's Chianti Classico Riserva, first produced in 1990 to mark Dievole's 900th anniversary. The menu follows a seasonal, ingredient-driven philosophy, incorporating wild herbs foraged from nearby fields, ancient grains and produce

Rinuccio 1180

from trusted local suppliers. Dishes reflect traditional Tuscan flavours reinterpreted, from handmade pasta, to fresh vegetables and grilled meats. In summer, meals are served in the Aione courtyard, surrounded by fragrant roses, while winter dining takes place in the warm, inviting rooms of an 18th-century villa. Adjacent to the restaurant, the Lounge Bar and Giardino del Tasso provide a relaxed setting for an aperitivo, overlooking the Sangiovese vineyards and olive groves.

dievole.it

Osteria di Passignano

Osteria di Passignano, Via Passignano 33, Loc. Badia a Passignano - 50028 - Tavarnelle Val di Pesa (FI)

Antinori's Osteria di Passignano is serenely situated between the vineyards of Chianti Classico, and is deeply connected to the historic Abbey of Passignano, a medieval monastery with a legacy in viticulture dating back over a thousand years. The restaurant sits in the shadow of this historic landmark, blending tradition with a contemporary approach to Tuscan cuisine. The menu focuses on seasonal ingredients, sourced from local producers and the surrounding countryside, with dishes designed to highlight

Where winemakers dine

In Peccioli, we love **La Dispensa**. Nora and Giacomo welcome you with a smile and you can taste Tuscan tradition within their refined, balanced and truly excellent dishes. The red wine risotto with black truffle is very popular as is the *bistecca* with grilled courgettes. There are more and more local wines on the menu too, with labels from Terre di Pisa DOC and the fruity Chianti Colline Pisane.

Francesco Lomi, Usiglian del Vescovo, Pisa

the flavours of the region and partner Antinori's portfolio of wines, particularly selections from the Badia a Passignano estate. The setting, with its vaulted stone interiors, views of the abbey's ancient walls and access to its herb gardens, provides an evocative connection to the history and winemaking heritage of the area.

osteriadipassignano.com

Il Pievano (Castello di Spaltenna)

Via Spaltenna, 13 - Località Pieve di Spaltenna - 53013 - Gaiole in Chianti (SIENA)

The one-thousand-year-old monastery at Castello di Spaltenna is an atmospheric setting for its restaurant. Il Pievano has held a Michelin star since 2017, offering a thoughtful balance of tradition and creativity. The restaurant's setting is as captivating as its cuisine, with dining available in the elegant Sala dei Papi or the tranquil inner courtyard. Greek-born chef Stelios Sakalis reinterprets both Tuscan and Greek flavours and crafts seasonal menus, including a surprise tasting menu, that highlight both regions from a contemporary perspective. Dishes such as acorn-flour pasta served with red prawns cooked with feta cheese, *saganaki*-style, showcase his innovative fusion, while a selection of refined starters and pastry desserts add to the experience. The wine list focuses on the castle's estate-grown Chianti Classico wines. Although Il Pievano closes for the off-season, throughout spring and summer it is easily one of the most important references in Chianti's fine-dining repertoire.

spaltenna.it

Osteria di Brolio (Ricasoli)

Loc. Madonna a Brolio - 53013 - Gaiole in Chianti (SI)

Castello di Brolio is another of Tuscan wine's legendary landmarks. The osteria, tucked into the landscape of Chianti Classico, just below the castle walls, blends tradition with modern creativity. The restaurant's setting, framed by vineyards and woodland, offers a relaxed yet polished dining space, where the focus is on high-quality seasonal ingredients sourced from local producers and the estate's own gardens. Under the direction of chef Franco Sangiacomo, the kitchen presents a menu that is inspired by the region's traditions and features the likes of creamy bean soups and sirloin steaks, while allowing room for inventive pairings, such as lamb ravioli with goat cheese and black garlic, local fallow deer with cherries and chocolate, or cuttlefish pie in chickpea sauce. Each dish is crafted to complement the wines of Ricasoli, from the structured Castello di Brolio Gran Selezione to the impressive Casalferro Merlot. With its balance of research, regionality and precision, Osteria di Brolio offers a dining experience that reflects the depth of Chianti Classico's food and wine culture.

ricasoli.com

MONTALCINO

Il Brunello (Castello di Velona)

Località La Velona - 53024 - Montalcino, Siena

Il Brunello is the signature restaurant of Castello di Velona, a hilltop estate overlooking the Val d'Orcia in the south of the region. Found within the original structure of the medieval castle, it offers a formal dining experience shaped by the traditions and ingredients of Montalcino and the nearby Amiata region. Set within the castle's original structure, the restaurant's stone walls, vaulted ceilings and panoramic terraces frame sweeping views of the Val d'Orcia. The menu follows a seasonal, ingredient-driven philosophy, blending Tuscan tradition with contemporary finesse. Estate-grown olive oil, wild herbs and carefully sourced regional ingredients shape elegantly plated dishes and tasting menus that balance rustic authenticity with Mediterranean influences. The wine list is deeply rooted in Brunello di Montalcino, including selections from the estate's own five hectares of vineyards. Great for couples sharing a bottle amidst white tablecloths, candlelight and an open fire.

castellodivelona.it

MONTEPULCIANO

Indigeno (Salcheto)

Via di Villa Bianca, 15 - 53045 -

Montepulciano (SI)

Salcheto's Montepulciano property is a must-stop for both its wines and Indigeno, the sustainable, forward-thinking on-site restaurant. Its design reflects the ethos of the winemaking – natural materials, minimal intervention and a seamless connection to the surrounding vineyards. The menu is centred on organic, locally sourced ingredients, with a strong emphasis on plant-based and low-impact dishes that chime with Salcheto's commitment to biodynamic viticulture. Given those values, the menu is extremely local, with game, courtyard geese and the freshwater fish of Montepulciano featuring prominently. The wine list focuses on Salcheto's Vino Nobile di Montepulciano and includes a range of no-sulphur-added wines. A very on-trend stop with a focus on sustainability.

salcheto.it/ospitalita/

Osteria Enoteca San Guido

BOLGHERI

Osteria Enoteca San Guido (Tenuta San Guido)

Osteria Enoteca San Guido, Località S. Guido, 50 - 57022 - Bolgheri (LI)

Situated in the heart of Bolgheri, Osteria Enoteca San Guido offers a rare opportunity to experience the wines of Tenuta San Guido alongside carefully curated dishes. Sassicaia may hog the headlines, but guests will no doubt find themselves enjoying other wines from the estate, such as Guidalberto and Le Difese, which provide insight into the broader winemaking philosophy of Tenuta San Guido. But the restaurant has a strong wine list showcasing nearby estates, as well as plenty of notable domaines from all over France. The space, which is also open for coffee and pastries, reflects the estate's understated elegance, with a rustic interior. The menu showcases local seafood, meats and seasonal produce presented in a contemporary style. While the cuisine is deliberately unfussy, the wine list is the true highlight; it even features a vertical selection of Sassicaia, one of the world's most celebrated wines. There's lots of quiet sophistication here.

enotecasanguido.com

Where winemakers dine

Among my favourite places is **Innocenti Wines** in Poggibonsi. It's the perfect synthesis of excellent cuisine with an incredible collection of bottles – certainly one of the most impressive wine lists in Siena. The dishes are a representation of the region, but there are always fresh and innovative offerings. The depth of regions available on the wine list is so great that one visit is not enough. And then it is close to one of the most fascinating places in Tuscany: San Gimignano, known in the world as the Manhattan of the Middle Ages. A place whose beauty seems to have frozen in time some 700 years ago, but with a beating contemporary heart.

Miria Bracali,
Famiglia Cecchi, Poggibonsi

Fine dining in Florence, Siena and Tuscany's great wine towns

The hillsides and plains of Tuscany are synonymous with wine-growing excellence, but they also furnish quality vegetables, prized truffles and prime meats. For centuries, these ingredients have been celebrated in a regional cuisine renowned for soups, pastas and steaks. Guidebooks will invariably refer to it as hearty, but the region's fine-dining establishments, which have proliferated in the last couple of decades, are here to counter any accusations that Tuscany's dishes are overly rich.

Osteria del Tasso

At award-winning restaurants and refined *osterie*, Tuscany's deep-rooted traditions of terroir give backbone to plates served with flair and finesse. Primary ingredients are often the stars of culinary creations, and many kitchens draw on nearby or on-site gardens and farms to supply them with zero-kilometre ingredients. Home-grown and international cheffing talent has brought avant-garde ideas to traditional haute-cuisine restaurants and has seen the opening of experimental new-wave restaurants, too.

And fine dining is not only flourishing in the elegant cities of Florence and Siena. Chefs are launching ventures in Tuscany's great wine towns, from Montepulciano to Montalcino, while an unassuming dirt track can lead to a two-starred Michelin *ristorante* and a celebrated *osteria* is an island among the Bolgheri vineyards. From these tables, there's always a feast for the eyes, too, whether it be Brunelleschi's pioneering dome of Florence Cathedral, a vine-garbed hillside or a distant glimpse of the Tyrrhenian Sea.

Ristorante Santa Elisabetta, Florence

Piazza Santa Elisabetta, 3 - 50122 Firenze
+39 055 2737673

Housed on the first floor of the byzantine Pagliazza Tower, Santa Elisabetta's seven tables are set in a circular stone-walled room illuminated by a chandelier. This exclusive two-Michelin-starred restaurant is headed up by chef Rocco De Santis who has dreamed up a minimalist cuisine exalting primary ingredients. Each dish has a 'protagonist' and is characterized by contrasts: cooked and raw; acidity and sweetness. On the menu you

Santa Elisabetha

Where winemakers dine

The place that has our heart is undoubtedly **Pasticceria Ferretti** in Peccioli, close to Libbiano. It's a place where you feel at home, founded more than 100 years ago. Lorella, the fourth generation of the Ferretti family, now runs the pastry shop that became a warm and welcoming restaurant, serving local food paired with a nice selection of wines. From breakfast to dinner, you can visit them and enjoy homemade quality products.

Nicola Cantoni,
Fattoria Fibbiano, Pisa

might find eel with yakitori, tosazu (dashi vinegar), almond and tarragon or smoked amberjack with Béarnaise sauce, Sorrento lemon jelly and celery.

ristorantesantaelisabetta.it/en/

Ristorante Atto di Vito Mollica, Florence

Palazzo Portinari Salviati
Via del Corso 6 – 50122 Firenze
+39 055 5353555

Dining in Ristorante Atto di Vito Mollica's fresco-adorned courtyard with its stained-glass roof and a tinkling fountain is a blissful experience. Housed inside the 15th-century Palazzo Portinari Salviati, the one-Michelin-starred restaurant's name means 'act' and each course arrives like an operatic masterpiece. Expect regal extravagance in dishes like scampi with a carrot and orange reduction and Champagne sauce, royal oyster with green apple soda and caviar, and hare à la royale with *dolceforte* (a sauce more traditionally served with wild boar in this part of Italy) and creamy red potatoes. The wine cellar has over 850 labels including historic brands and small producers from the Tuscany region.

attodivitomollica.com/ristorante-atto-di-vito-mollica-firenze/

Ristorante Atto di Vito Mollica

Saporium Firenze, Florence

Lungarno Benvenuto Cellini,
63/R, 50125 Firenze
+39 055 212933

The city offshoot of Borgo Santo Pietro Saporium, found in the Sienese countryside, upholds the same principles of biodiversity and regenerative agriculture as the rural retreat, earning it a Michelin Green star for sustainability. Vegetables, herbs, honey and cheese come from the nearby organic farm and fermented foods from an in-house laboratory. Chef Ariel Hagen's team includes a master gardener, a forager, a cheesemaker and a fermentation specialist. The resulting 'earth to table' dishes, from snails with grilled chicory and Tuscan garlic to rice with turnip tops and sheep kefir, look like exquisite miniature gardens.

saporium.com/it/firenze/

Angel Roofbar & Dining, Florence

Calimala Florence
Via Calimala, 2 - 50123 Firenze
+39 055 093 6360

If Florence's supreme elegance gets a little overbearing, loosen up at Angel on the top floor of Hotel Calimala. Though located in the heart of the historic quarter, surrounded by time-honoured fashion houses, the property is a buzzy, art deco-inspired venture injecting some cool into Florence's occasionally haughty haute cuisine. In the indoor, bare-brick dining room there is regular live music while the outdoor terrace has lofty views of the city's marble-clad Duomo. Chef Noam Huber serves a Mediterranean-Middle Eastern fusion. Expect roasted aubergine with fennel leaves on Lebanese milk bread, sashimi with tomato gazpacho and fermented chilli oil, and toasted

Angel

ciabatta bread with tartare of 25-day dry-aged beef tenderloin and a date-infused demi-glace.

angelroofbar.com/

Campo Cedro, Siena

Via Pian D'Ovile, 54 - 53100 Siena
+39 0577 236027

At Campo Cedro, located just off the tourist-beaten track of Siena, Japanese chef Kohsuke Sugihara brings the delicacy and artistry of food presentation from his homeland and applies it to Italian cuisine. With the plate as his canvas, his ingredients are modelled into dainty forms and colourful displays. Dishes include veal tongue millefeuille with caciocavallo cheese and black cabbage, puffed rice crusted croaker fish with seaweed sauce, and pumpkin and white chocolate cake with masala chai ice cream.

campocedro.com/

Particolare di Siena, Siena

Via Baldassarre Peruzzi, 26, 53100 Siena
+39 339 827 5430

Diners can choose from a series of evocative settings at Particolare di Siena. Its vaulted hall features cotto-tiled arches or there's a cavern with rough stone walls lit up dramatically and a cellar lined with bottles in illuminated diamond-pattern shelving. The food is a modern, fresh take on the regional cuisine using locally sourced ingredients. The fish menu features red prawns with roasted datterino tomatoes and sun-dried orange, and octopus with leeks, olive dust and *salmoriglio* (a Sicilian lemon sauce), while meat options include Chianina beef carpaccio with olives, capers, mustard mayonnaise or a low-temperature cooked pork shank with Jerusalem artichoke, green apple, spices and Vin Santo sauce.

particolaredisiena.com/

Ristorante Campo del Drago, Montalcino

53024 Castiglion del Bosco, Siena
+39 0577 191 3135

Two-Michelin-starred Campo del Drago is a masterclass in classic fine dining hidden down a country lane inside the Rosewood Hotel's Castiglion del Bosco resort. Before a view of vineyard-draped hills and shadowy mountains, diners indulge in course after course of painterly-plated contemporary Tuscan cuisine. Under executive chef Matteo Temperini, the kitchen serves up exquisite dishes of eel with smoked yoghurt and carrots from the estate, blue lobster with samphire and limoncello, and venison ravioli with octopus water and sea fennel.

rosewoodhotels.com/it/castiglion-del-bosco/dining/ristorante-campo-del-drago

Le Logge del Vignola, Montepulciano

Via dell'Erbe, 6 IT- 53045 Montepulciano
+39 0578 717290

Montepulciano is a monument to medieval majesty with a crenelated municipal hall and steep, shaded streets. Along one stone-flagged incline is Le Logge del Vignola, with a softly lit, brick-walled interior and tiny terrace outside. The bright dishes arrive at the table with a theatrical flourish – a garnish of smoke, a swirl of sauce or a brief moment aflame. Classics are reinvented, like chicken liver pâté enlivened with coffee bread and a spiced pear and wine sauce, or ribollita soup refined by a black cabbage and black chickpea puff pastry crust.

leloggedelvignola.com/en/

Le Logge del Vignola

Where winemakers dine

Osteria l'Ciocio is a true advocate for the region's high-quality food and wine culture. The restaurant offers dishes that celebrate tradition alongside original reinterpretations, with meticulous attention to the quality and sustainability of raw ingredients, service and the wine selection. In addition to a wonderful selection of meats, one of our favourite dishes is marinated palamita fish with miso, grilled to perfection. With our Japanese roots, we can only appreciate this fusion of the Tuscan coast and the Orient.

Hideyuki Miyakawa, Bulichella, Suvereto

Osteria del Tasso, Bolgheri

Via Bolgherese km 3.9, Località San Walfredo 184/A
57020 Bolgheri
+39 0565 182 8061

Osteria del Tasso offers indoor dining in an elegantly restored barn with plum-coloured walls or outside in tree-shaded gardens encircled by Bolgheri vineyards. The food is a contemporary reinterpretation of dishes from the territory, with several revived recipes belonging to the Antinori family. Adapted from the great winemaking family's cookbook are marinated anchovies with Tropea onions, tomatoes and crispy bread, and agnolotto pasta stuffed with three roast meats and served with parmesan fondue and black truffle. Ingredients sourced from the onsite farm are highlighted on the menu, from fallow deer carpaccio to pork ribs served with tempura vegetables. The accompanying wine list has dozens of labels from the onsite Antinori-owned Tenuta Guado al Tasso including its homonymous Bolgheri Superiore DOC, with vintages heading as far back as 2001.

osteriadeltasso.com/

Osteria del Tasso

Ristorante Biagio Pignatta, Carmignano (Prato province)

Viale Papa Giovanni XXIII,
59015 Artimino PO, Italy
+39 055 875 1406

Presided over by a monumental Medici hunting lodge from the 16th century (guided tours available), Tenuta di Artimino houses guests in the restored 17th-century stables. A short walk away, dinner is served at Biagio Pignatta, named after Ferdinando I de Medici's butler. Chef Michela Bottasso has a passion for delving into historic recipe books. Her menu includes dishes like duck breast with carrots, star anise and orange, which recalls the duck à l'orange that Italian-born Catherine de Medici brought to France when she married King Henry II.

melia.com/it/hotels/italia/firenze/hotel-tenuta-di-artimino-melia-collection/ristoranti/biagio-pignatta

La Rocca, Montaione (Florence province)

Loc Castelfalfi, 50050 Montaione, Firenze
+390571892000

Castelfalfi is a historic hamlet turned resort surrounded by nature's bounty; organic vineyards, olive groves, vegetable plots and beehives provide scenic grounds for guests and prime produce for the kitchens. At La Rocca, meaning 'fortress' and named for its location inside the medieval castle, chef Davide De Simone dishes up an aromatic, seasonally inspired cuisine that echoes the colours and scents of nature. The menu includes venison ravioli with sea urchin, turbot with truffle and mandarin, and pear with chocolate, hibiscus and Sichuan pepper.

castelfalfi.com/la-rocca-di-castelfalfi

Vegan Agrivilla I Pini, San Gimignano

Loc Santa Margherita, 37, 53037 San Gimignano SI, Italy
+39 0577 940650

Vegan Agrivilla I Pini is situated in the valley just below San Gimignano, whose medieval 'skyscrapers' crown the horizon. Despite the health retreat-esque name, the property with its earthy-toned elegance is much more about laid-back, rural luxury. Wellness and mindful eating are seen as an indulgence, not a restriction here. The restaurant is 100% plant-based with a seed-to-table philosophy, but you won't just be picking through lettuce leaves. The fresh, artfully plated dishes by 'Lahiri the Vegan Chef' (who goes by this online moniker) include a hot-pink beetroot gazpacho with garlic pesto and pasta parcels stuffed with chard and almond ricotta.

ipinitoscana.com/en/vegan-restaurant-p9.html

Lux Lucis, Forte dei Marmi

Viale Ammiraglio Morin 6755042 Forte dei Marmi (Lucca)
+39 0584 783636

Situated on the rooftop of Hotel Principe Forte dei Marmi, Lux Lucis boasts floor-to-

ceiling windows overlooking a landscape caught between the Apuan Alps and the Tyrrhenian Sea. Modena-born chef Valentino Cassanelli describes his food as a 'free expression of Italian cuisine' with an emphasis on the suppliers and products of the surrounding territory. Drawing from both land and sea, his dishes include roasted scallop with lamb brain, *fichimole* (guacamole of figs) and turnip tops, wild duck with banana, horseradish and olives, and risotto with pumpkin *saor* (a Venetian vinegar and onion dressing), Tuscan *soppressata* (cured sausage) and barley. The restaurant has a new wine cellar ready for its seasonal reopening in April, with a particular focus on small, local producers.

principefortedeimarmi.com/en/dining/lux-lucis/

Osteria La Dritta, Lucca

Piazza S.Francesco, 33, 55100 Lucca

+39 377 363 3781

Located in the historic centre of Lucca, a city just a beat from Chianti land, La Dritta styles itself as a new-age *osteria*. You'll find classic dishes like stuffed pasta, bean soups and steaks restyled with a creative, modern touch. The menu includes the prettily-plated millefeuille of potatoes topped with stracciatella cheese and onion, ditali pasta with beans and tiger prawns, and radicchio with leek confit and goat's cheese. La Dritta recently came first place in Italy's televised culinary competition '4 Ristoranti'.

osterialadritta.eatbu.com/

Where to find the best aperitivo in Florence

As the birthplace of the Negroni and with the Chianti region on the doorstep, drinking in Florence is a pretty prestigious pastime. But aperitivo hour here is as much about the snacks as it is the drinks. Phoebe Hunt takes us on a crawl through Florence's cobbled streets and lively piazzas to ten of the best bars for partaking in the food-and-drink tradition.

Bulli e Balene

Aperitivo is a practice so central to Italian social lives, it's hard to define; not least because it can be interpreted in so many different ways. It is the golden hour that marks the transition from late afternoon to early evening, a time to pause with friends over a drink and something deliciously salty to snack on. In Florence, anything goes, from a handful of crisps to a lavish *tagliere* (charcuterie platter) piled high with Tuscan salami, local cheeses, *schiacciata* bread, olives and more. Aperitivo in Florence can also morph into a full-blown buffet dinner, known as '*apericena*', popular with students on a budget as a way to fill up on cheap fried carbs.

On every corner of the historic centre, you'll find blackboards touting €5 Spritz with bruschetta. While tempting, these are not strictly local to Florence. 'The most Florentine aperitivo you'll get is a glass of wine with a platter of *coccoli* (deep-fried dough balls), *stracchino* (soft, tangy cream cheese) and *prosciutto,*' says Francesco Mannarino, a trained sommelier who has lived in the city all his life. 'A *fiasco* of Chianti Classico between friends is delicious and cheap, and it's as local as it gets.'

Still, Florentines aren't afraid to branch out once in a while. Florence Cocktail Week – the eighth edition of which will take place from 7-13 April 2025 – has done a lot to encourage innovation in the city's most established bars. Across seven days, pop-up bars, mixology masterclasses, cocktail tastings, parties and guest shifts will shine a light on the city's evolving cocktail scene.

And of course, no story about Florentine aperitivi would be complete without a mention of the Negroni. This potent mix of gin, sweet vermouth and Campari was famously invented here at the request of Count Camillo Negroni in 1919. Bitter and bold, it's the ultimate pre-dinner cocktail and perhaps the reason food is so necessary when drinking in the city.

For a casual aperitivo crawl, you could simply head to the lively student haunts around Sant'Ambrogio and Borgo La Croce, where you can hop from bar to bar, sampling drinks and snacks along the way. Otherwise, map out your movements via this selection of the best local spots for an aperitivo in Florence.

Bulli e Balene

Via dello Sprone, 14/R

There's a lot to love about this tiny Venetian-inspired bar, tucked away in vibrant Piazza della Passerà (literally meaning 'Pussy Square' – Florence's historic red light district), but a €4 Spritz served in crystal-cut highball glasses is a good place to start. Aside from Aperol, they serve six or seven other Spritzes made using lesser-known bitter-orange aperitifs, as well as a refreshing elderflower Hugo Spritz for hot August nights. Drinks are served with delicious cicchetti snacks on toast – again taking a cue from Venice – with toppings including prosciutto, burrata, artichoke and red pepper.

What to drink: A Cynar Spritz – a version of the sparkling drink featuring the Italian digestivo, Cynar, which is made from artichokes (don't worry, you'd never guess)

facebook.com/bulliebalene

Caffè Gilli

Via Roma, 1r

Florence is home to the Negroni, famously created in 1919 when Count Camillo Negroni asked his bartender, Fosco Scarselli, to strengthen his favourite Milano-Torino by adding gin to the drink. Over one hundred

Caffè Gilli

years later and it's still a staple in the city (and known the world over), the ultimate aperitivo drink – where crisps and olives on the side are obligatory. In magnificent Piazza della Repubblica, close to the bar where the cocktail was first concocted, 270-year-old Caffè Gilli's Negronis come strong and perfectly proportioned.

What to drink: The Negroni (well, it would be rude not to)

caffegilli.com

Vineria Sonora

Via degli Alfani, 39r

A natural wine bar that wouldn't be out of place in east London, this chic spot near the Duomo prides itself on an exclusively

Italian collection of organic and biodynamic wines. These are served with aperitivo nibbles like fat Tuscan olives, *grissini* and grilled cheese toasties with onion marmalade. Perch at one of the high tables outside on a warm evening, or head inside to enjoy whatever's on the record player as you quaff your wine.

What to drink: One of the weekly changing orange wines available by the glass

vineriasonora.it

Enoteca Alla Sosta dei Papi

Borgo la Croce 81r

This is among the last of a dying breed of sweet and old-fashioned *enoteche* – a bottle shop meets wine tavern – with wooden barrels on display and kitsch bunches of plastic grapes hanging in the entrance. Florentines of all ages have a strong affinity for places like Sosta dei Papi, where you'll find deeply affordable Chianti Classico sold at near-cost price by the litre. Fill your glass and sit in with a platter of *coccoli*, *stracchino* and *prosciutto*, or fill up your own glass bottles to take home.

What to drink: A few glasses of the house wine

sostadeipapi.it

Where winemakers dine

One of the best restaurants in Suvereto is Moira Serini and Marco Ticciati's **Dal Cacini**. They only serve fresh fish, and only those found at the morning market. There's also a seven-course seafood menu served up in an intimate and private space. The typical pairing is with Vermentino, but let's not forget the native Ansonica – or why not a Sangiovese or Syrah rosé?

Giovanni Frascolla, Tua Rita, Suvereto

Cibrèo Caffè

Cibrèo Caffè

Via dei Pescioni, 8r

For aperitivi and people-watching with a difference, head to Cibrèo Caffè's swanky bar, lined with pot plants and vintage-striped banquettes, at the Helvetia & Bristol, one of Florence's most historic hotels. The freshly made Peach Bellini or a Rossini made with crushed strawberries and Prosecco (the latter only on the menu in spring and summer months) are to die for. Snacks include artisanal sourdough dunked in a Greek-inspired *skordalia* dip made from almonds and olive oil.

What to drink: The Peach Bellini

cibreo.com

Procacci 1885

Via Tornabuoni, 64r

This might just be the most civilized aperitivo hour you'll come across, especially in the colder months, when you can sit among Florentine old-timers in their fur coats and hats and watch the world go by. Come for the elegant art-deco interiors and impressive Antinori wine list; stay for the bitesize truffle buns – a delightful start to any evening. Tourists in trainers or T-shirts will definitely be looked down upon here, but there's nowhere quite like it.

What to drink: A glass of Marchese Antinori wine with a truffle bun – they have a 2021 Tignanello on the list, if you really want to push the boat out

procacci1885.it

Meno, Vini e Altre Necessità

Viale Aleardo Aleardi, 13R

Amid a sea of new openings offering more and more drinking options, and aiming to appeal to more and more tourists, Meno is decidedly different. Its name translates to 'less', and its owner – a Florentine who spent 25 years living in Puglia – explains that the aim is to make a return to simplicity; doing a few things and doing them well. As such, you'll find a small list

Meno, Vini e Altre Necessità

of wines from low-intervention and under-the-radar Italian producers, written on a chalkboard and changing often. In large, aperitivo snacks are inspired by Salento on Puglia's southern tip: think caciocavallo cheese, *panzerotti* (stuffed and deep-fried dough parcels) and moreish *taralli* biscuits.

What to drink: Ask owner Massimo for his recommendation from the Italian natural wines on offer and he'll likely let you try a couple of his favourites on the house before you make up your mind

instagram.com/meno_vini_ealtrenecessita/

Il Santino

Via di Santo Spirito, 60

Aperitivo-goers spill out onto the street from this tiny wine bar on a warm summer's evening, the hours slipping pleasantly away over a bottle of Brunello and some platters of *crostini*. A former wine cellar, Il Santino is run by the same trio behind the larger Il Santo Bevitore restaurant just two doors down. The wine list has about 200 labels, with a focus on small producers and, lately, a good selection of low-intervention wines. On cooler nights, perch at one of the four tiny tables or along the marble bar, where cured meats hang on hooks ready to be sliced up and served.

What to drink: Opt for one of the dozen or so wines by the glass, which are served with complimentary *crostini*

ilsantobevitore.com

Il Santino

Locale

Via delle Seggiole 12r

This Medici palace turned late-night drinking den strikes the delicate balance between louche all-night parties and world-class mixology, and is hands down the coolest cocktail spot in town. Each season, head bartender Alessandro Mengoni picks three local ingredients – pumpkin, peach and cucumber, for example – and concocts a drinks menu around them. For aperitivo, you'll get a carefully balanced tower of avant-garde nibbles like polenta chips with lacto-fermented radicchio and a beignet with olives, mushrooms and green lentil foam. The clientele is made up of high-energy Italian socialites, with sequins and corsets the unspoken dress code on weekends – dancing on tables isn't unheard of.

What to drink: The cocktail menu changes with the seasons, but certain staples such as the Mezcal Negroni, made with kombucha vermouth and saffron, are perennial favourites

localefirenze.it

Locale

Where winemakers dine

If you don't finish your sandwich at **Bar Trombetta**, you may get a piercing look from the owner. Trombetta is a side-of-the-road bar that looks quite innocuous – until you take a closer look. Then you see, on the stripy canopy over the entrance, what is probably the world's greatest logo: a wild boar being fired out of a trumpet. Dining is a whirlwind of carefully sourced porchetta, pancetta and *acciughe* (anchovies) – all served between two simple slices of bread. The porchetta is the centrepiece and in Tuscany, at least, there is no better slice. When you catch it still lukewarm, it is particularly good – but everything available is worth having a shot at.

James Marshall-Lockyer, Tenuta Licina, Arezzo

Bulli e Balene

The best trattorias in Tuscany

Chequered tablecloths, hand-written menus and straw-wrapped *fiascos* of red wine... the trattoria is a gateway to authentic, delicious, age-old Tuscan cooking.

Antica Macelleria Cecchini

Deeply rooted in rural traditions and subsistence farming, Tuscan food is hearty, seasonal and unpretentious. It's often referred to as *la cucina povera*, peasant cooking, with plenty of offal, stews and humble garden vegetables. The northern regions call the Tuscans 'bean-eaters', mocking the regional obsession with pulses and legumes. And while this is true, Tuscany's cuisine is much more than that.

Take *peposo*, for example, a robust beef and peppercorn stew that was invented in the 1400s in the village of Impruneta and cooked in the ovens used to bake the terracotta tiles atop the Florence Duomo. Visit any old-fashioned trattoria in Tuscany in winter, and you're likely to find this same ancient dish on the menu. *Bistecca Fiorentina*, or Florentine steak, is another such example, said to have its origins around the 1500s when medieval knights from England were passing through Florence and requested 'beef steak', which was then adapted to the word 'bistecca'.

The cosy trattoria – less formal than a restaurant, but more substantial than the snacky, wine-focused osteria – is a gateway into these authentic, delicious and age-old Tuscan dishes. We're talking family-run establishments with chequered tablecloths, hand-written menus and straw-wrapped *fiascos* of red wine on the table.

Trattoria Cammillo, Florence

Borgo San Jacopo 57r, Florence; +39 055 212427

In a city overrun by tourists, Cammillo remains reassuringly unchanged by the whims and trends of the moment. This family-run trattoria is one of Florence's most iconic and has been a stalwart on Florence's dining scene since 1945. Today, it's still run by Cammillo's granddaughter, Chiara, who you'll often spot greeting guests like old friends and checking everything is shipshape. The restaurant is made up of several small dining rooms; opt for the main room at the entrance for the best atmosphere. While it's more expensive than some other trattorias, the outstanding daily specials – light-as-a-feather fried courgette flowers, handmade tagliatelle with fresh porcini mushrooms, tagliarini in a ham and artichoke sauce, or *baccalà alla Livornese* (a traditional salt cod dish) – are invariably worth it.

Vini e Vecchi Sapori, Florence

Via dei Magazzini, 3r, Florence; +39 055 293045

In general, the best rustic trattorias are found tucked down cobbled side streets or outside the city centre, away from the main thoroughfares and piazzas. Not so with Vini e Vecchi Sapori, which bucks the trend and is hidden in plain sight in one of Florence's most touristy squares: Piazza della Signoria. It's just a short saunter from the Uffizi Galleries and the Duomo, and inside the walls are clad with rows of wine bottles, old newspaper clippings and black and white photos of Florence in days gone by. The food, served at well-worn wooden tables, is simple and exquisite: piles of thick tagliatelle with slow-cooked duck ragù, tripe, grilled lamb cutlets, and their famous saffron and courgette flower pasta throughout the summer months. For pudding, raspberry tiramisu hits the spot every time, washed down with a shot glass of raspberry-infused grappa.

vini-e-vecchi-sapori.restaurants-world.com/

Trattoria Cibrèo, Florence

Via Andrea del Verrocchio, 8r, Florence; +39 055 234 1100

Cibrèo is named after a humble and almost-forgotten Tuscan peasant dish, made from chicken combs, cockscomb and wattle (the fleshy hanging part

Vine e Vecchi Sapori

under the beak). Though they rarely serve this exact offal dish on the menu, the trattoria stays true to its roots in bringing Tuscan countryside traditions to the vibrant market quarter of Sant'Ambrogio. Founded in 1979 by Fabio Picchi and now run by his son Giulio, the trattoria is an homage to a disappearing way of rural life in the countryside around Florence. Many restaurants claim to have a 'strong focus on produce', but with the market literally metres away, Cibrèo is a place where you can really taste this: the freshest summer tomatoes made into a sensational *gelatina*, drizzled with grassy olive oil, or the first spring globe artichokes served '*alla mamma*' over buttery potato purée and a confit egg yolk. For a more formal dining experience, the adjacent ristorante serves up a similar concept from the same kitchen, but with a culinary finesse, white tablecloths and a price point to suit.

cibreo.com/sant-ambrogio/trattoria

Trattoria Cibrèo

Trattoria La Casa del Prosciutto, Vicchio

Via Ponte a Vicchio, 1, 50039 Vicchio; +39 055 844031

While most tourists head south of Florence towards Chianti, the northeastern rolling hills of Mugello have beautiful scenery and produce with a fraction of the visitors. Perched on the edge of a river, Casa del Prosciutto serves fantastic cured meats (as the name suggests) but also great pasta dishes and wines from a range of tiny producers. Service is slapdash and familial, and the interiors are all wood-clad walls and red chequered tablecloths. After eating your fill, enjoy an amaro or grappa at the bar, before a stroll (or cooling dip) along the nearby river.

casadelprosciutto.it/

L'Osteria di Casa Chianti, Certaldo

Via Lucardese, 82, 50052 Certaldo; +39 0571 669688

Get away from the crowds and take the train from Florence to the sleepy, little-visited town of Certaldo for lunch in the countryside. Once here, hike or take a short taxi into the hills to L'Osteria di Casa Chianti, a true old-school establishment that's been run by the same family for decades. While they do serve excellent wines, Casa Chianti isn't part of a vineyard, and instead serves wines from across Tuscany and beyond. The bread is baked each day in a traditional wood oven and the pasta made by hand, drizzled with exquisite grassy olive oil made from their own olives. If you like what you try, the olive oil is available to take home by the litre too.

osteriadicasachianti.it/

Da Delfina, Montalbano

Via della Chiesa, 1, 59015 Artimino; +39 055 871 8074

In the small village of Artimino – less than an hour's drive from Florence – Da Delfina is a classic Sunday lunch spot for Florentines and tourists alike. This is the kind of place you order antipasti, primi, secondi *and* dolci, lingering over each course and rolling out many hours later. The menu is short and meat-heavy: feast on rabbit, wild boar, bistecca, crostini misti and vegetables from the land, saving room for the somewhat legendary rice pudding served with lashings of orange marmalade. In spring and summer, the terrace of this crumbling Medici-era villa is impossibly picturesque, gazing out onto olive groves and the rolling Montalbano hills below. In winter, sit inside by the fire, enjoying the smell of meat cooking slowly over the grill. Owner Carlo Cioni took this place over from his mother Delfina, and is passionate about the history of this little slice of countryside and its *cucina povera* (or so-called peasant-cooking) traditions.

dadelfina.it/

Mangiando Mangiando, Greve in Chianti

Piazza Giacomo Matteotti, 80, 50022 Greve in Chianti; +39 055 854 6372

The sweet market town of Greve in Chianti is a mainstay on the Tuscan vineyard circuit, and well-located for many winery tours. Soak up all the drinking with a hearty meal at Mangiando Mangiando (which translates to 'eating, eating'), a laid-back trattoria located right

Mangiando Mangiando

in the central piazza. Platters of cured meats and crostini are generous in size, as are the pasta dishes. Peposo, the slow-cooked peppercorn beef stew originating in the nearby village of Impruneta, is cooked in Chianti Classico wine and served with potatoes and cannellini beans *al forno*.

mangiandomangiando.it/

Antica Macelleria Cecchini, Panzano

Via XX Luglio, 11, 50022 Panzano in Chianti, Greve in Chianti; +39 055 852020

Made famous by Chef's Table on Netflix, this old butchers-meets-restaurant has shot into the spotlight over the last few years. Aside from making bookings a little harder to come by, very little has changed: charismatic and larger-than-life owner Dario Cecchini, an eighth-generation butcher with a palpable passion for his work, is still there reciting Dante and guffawing away as he chats to guests. The menu is a celebration of Tuscan beef, nose-to-tail cooking before it became cool. Start with an aperitivo drink and snack in the adjacent butcher-shop before heading through to long, communal tables. A large bottle of house Chianti is plonked on the table, essentially bottomless, as you're taken through different cuts and styles of beef, as well as other meat dishes in the heart of the Chianti region. Dario is known not only for his masterful butchery but also for his deep respect for the animals he prepares, and this is one of the best places in Tuscany for a spot of steak indulgence.

dariocecchini.com

La Bottega di Elena

La Bottega di Elena, Bolgheri

Strada Giulia, 2, 57022 Bolgheri; +39 0565 762141

Bolgheri town is in the heart of prime wine country, surrounded by Super-Tuscan vineyards. Perched on top of a hill inside medieval ramparts, this idyllic walled village is also an underrated foodie hotspot, with access to the best sun-drenched produce but also just a few miles from the Tyrrhenian Sea. For a casual lunch after strolling around the village, make a beeline for La Bottega di Elena, a great casual spot in the very centre. Don't skimp on the antipasti – giant platters of crostini topped with *fegato* (liver pâté) and lardo, artisanal cheeses and an array of cold cut meats. The handwritten menu features hyper-regional dishes like pici with ragù, Livornese-style tripe and giant chickpeas with anchovies, drowned in olive oil.

La Capanna dello Zio Tom, Castiglioncello

Via delQuercetano 1/c, Castiglioncello; +39 334 397 4542

There are no chequered tablecloths and cosy wood-clad corners at La Capanna dello Zio Tom. Instead, this trattoria comes and goes with the seasons, erected each spring just metres from the beach at Castiglioncello. Throughout the summer months, swimmers and sunbathers stroll up here after a morning on the beach to savour the freshest *fritti di mare* and seafood pasta, enjoyed to the sound of the waves and the occasional pesky seagull. Yet despite the al fresco vibes, those quintessential hallmarks of a classic Tuscan trattoria remain: hearty portions, unpretentious service, paper tablecloths, bitter espressos and homely cooking are all here in abundance.

L'antica Venezia, Livorno

Piazza Dei Domenicani 15, Livorno; +39 0586 887353

The Renaissance port city of Livorno is often overlooked by tourists in favour of Pisa, but those who do venture here will discover a rich and unique culinary heritage. Alongside all the classic Tuscan dishes, the cuisine is influenced by centuries of trade with the Ottoman Empire and beyond, as well as flavours from up and down the French-Italian coastline. Tucked away by the canals, the family-run Trattoria L'antica Venezia is a diamond in the rough. On a summer's evening, bag one of the trestle tables outside and dive into plates of *fritti misti* – an assortment of local deep-fried seafood – followed by *spaghetti alla vongole* piled high with buttery clams, parsley and grated lemon zest. This is also *the* place to try *baccalà alla Livornese*, Livorno's signature salted cod, lightly breaded and served with summer tomatoes and onions. The menu changes depending on the catch of the day and is written on a chalkboard that fills the main wall inside.

Arduino Osteria Ancestrale, Castagneto Carducci

loc. Magazzino, 57022 Castagneto Carducci; +39 324 903 1810

Arduino offers traditional Tuscan cooking with a contemporary edge, located in the hills near Castagneto Carducci and not far from Bolgheri. The farm-to-table osteria is a labour of love from young couple Fabrizio and Martina, who left the city and returned to Fabrizio's family farm to open their own place. But rather than opening yet another agriturismo, they've taken regenerative farm-to-table cooking to new and exciting places. Figs, onions, tomatoes, fennel, beetroot and plum, all grown here, are not simply made into jams and pasta sauces. Instead, you'll sample onion stalk (usually discarded) piped with basil and lemon granita, a shot of fig leaf infusion, a plum sambal. There's no fixed menu, but the food is almost always vegetarian and primarily cooked over fire. Despite the culinary creativity, the decor is rustic yet elegant, with a warm

Arduino Osteria Ancestrale

atmosphere that feels like stepping into a Tuscan home. Arrive early and have a stroll around the eight hectares of organically farmed land, with a vineyard, four varieties of olive trees, hundreds of fruit trees and animals grazing.

poderearduino.com/osteria-ancestrale-ita/

Teatro del Mare, Piombino

Piazza Giovanni Bovio 5, Piombino; +39 0565 49346

Piombino is usually a stopping-off point on the way to the island of Elba, but if you find yourself in need of a good lunch before travelling then you're in luck with Teatro del Mare. This excellent trattoria is tucked down by the water in the heart of the historic harbour, so close that you feel like you're on a boat. Translated as 'theatre of the sea', the main attraction is its historic waterfront setting, but the food more than lives up to the views of the boats coming in and out. Prices are in line with the market catch of the day, and giant langoustine, cod, mackerel and anchovies all find their way onto the menu. The trattoria is a short drive from the modern ferry port over to Elba and also a cordoned-off swimming area where you can take a cooling dip after lunch.

Teatrodelmare.com

Teatro del Mare

Trattoria Cammillo

The best enotecas in Tuscany

Look up the word '*teca*' in the Italian dictionary and you'll find it defined as a 'highly decorated case for displaying holy things'. In Italy, this takes form in the country's many *-teca*: there's the temple to books, the *biblioteca*, or the place to play with collections of games, the *ludoteca*. And then, of course, there's the shrine to wine, the *enoteca*.

La Vecchia Nicchia

In every town in Tuscany one can find an *enoteca* – a relaxed, welcoming wine shop far more characterful than the supermarket and geared towards buying local wines. Some *enoteche* (the Italian plural), however, have a more extensive offering in terms of their wine selection – reaching outside the region's borders, showcasing wines from other parts of Italy and the rest of the world.

Crucially, at these idiosyncratic Italian wine shops there is often the added bonus of customer interaction; a chat with the owner to understand what might be the best bottle for a gift, or for the evening's meal. There may also be the opportunity to take a seat and taste the wines – to open a bottle for a few euros more than the shelf price or enjoy a wine by the glass. And because this is Italy, where there is the unspoken understanding that wine is best enjoyed at the dining table, you can often find food being served too, from simple plates of cured meats and cheeses to four-course menus. Do call ahead to check if this is the case; but if not, head out armed with a corkscrew. That way, you can take your bottle across the road, grab a sandwich from the *paninoteca* and have yourself a *grande picnic*.

Here below are the best shops for wine buying in Tuscany.

Enoteca Rivella

Viale Camillo Benso di Cavour, 86, Siena
+39 0577 47344

From the historic centre of Siena, walk through the neighbourhood of the Porcupine (la contrada sovrana dell'Istrice) and exit at the northern gate, Porta Camollia, to reach this brilliant wine shop. Enoteca Rivella is hidden behind a curtain of corks and cigar smoke. The owner, Carlo Bottiglioni, is never seen smoking, but the mysterious aroma lends the shop the atmosphere of an old library, aided further by the fact that it is also rather dusty and dimly lit. The selection of wines is exquisite: Bottiglioni studied enology before opening his shop and his choices reflect a passion for authentic and profound wines. There are boxes half unpacked, sold before they can be put out on the shelves, like the Luna Sangiovese from Toru Oikawa, and bottles that look like they may have been relaxing a while in the company of their gentle owner; bottles with lesser-known labels and a tiny production. If they have earned a place at Enoteca Rivella, they are well worth investing in and trying. While in the neighbourhood, be sure to make a quick stop at Pasticceria Buti for a coffee and their famous *caramellato*, a lightly crunchy pastry filled with Italian Chantilly cream.

Formaggioteca Terroir

Via dei Renai, 19, Florence

When in Florence, do be sure to cross over the Arno River, for as well as discovering the artisan shoemakers and the house of Elizabeth Barrett Browning, you'll be rewarded with cheese. Find the most wonderful assortment, aged in a Chianti farmhouse and sold in the San Niccolò neighbourhood by husband-and-wife team Pierre and Rebecca Gouttenoire. Pecorino can often feel like the only variety to show up on cheeseboards in the region, served with the saltless *pane Toscano*. So when you arrive at Formaggioteca, you have to pinch yourself: those really are blue veins (try the Sasso Forte, the shop's own Italian take on Roquefort). The wine selection is just as refreshing. Pierre – who worked as a winemaker in Bordeaux for 15 years before starting a life with Rebecca in Tuscany (whom he met on a wine tour she was leading) – champions Crémant over Champagne, and the shelves are replete with some great bubbles from Savoie, Jura, Alsace and Burgundy. Rebecca, originally from Denmark, is an Italian Wine Scholar and continues to run wine tours from Florence into the famous wine regions nearby. Thus, on the shelves you'll also find the likes of Brunello producers Le Chiuse and San Polino.

formaggiotecaterroir.it

Formaggioteca Terroir

Enoteca Baldi

Enoteca Baldi

Piazza Gastone Bucciarelli, 25, Chianti

In the heart of the Chianti Classico, next to the famous butcher Dario Cecchini, is this wine shop and informal restaurant run by ex-River Cafe London staff, the Baldi sisters. Francesca works in the kitchen and Eleonora front of house with her partner Gianmaria Garbin, the wine buyer and sommelier. Wines can be pulled from the list for a few euros more than their takeaway price to be enjoyed with *antipasti*, *primi* and *secondi* from the short and sweet menu. The wine list is sweet too, but by no means short. It is extensive but not excessive, featuring the greatest names within the 11 Classico subzones before extending to include the best producers within Italy and the rest of the world. It is a joy to sit and drink from the extensive local selection and enjoy tasting flights from around the

Where winemakers dine

Among the many restaurants in Montalcino, my choice undoubtedly falls on **Trattoria Il Pozzo** in Sant'Angelo in Colle, managed by the same family for over thirty years. Fresh pasta (strictly homemade), vegetables from the local garden, seasonal berries and the best local meat make it the ideal place to take your time and savour Tuscan flavours in a truly familial atmosphere. All of this is complemented by a wide selection of local wines, with a clear emphasis on Sangiovese and the various expressions of Brunello di Montalcino.

Alessio Sostegni,
Poggio Antico,
Montalcino

region – particularly from a new wave of young producers, from Sophie Conte at Fattoria Tregole to Giacomo Baraldo in San Casciano dei Bagni. But it is perhaps the range of wines from Champagne, Loire, Burgundy and California that draws in the surrounding winemakers – do not be surprised to find yourself at a table next to superstar producers Giovanni Manetti of Fontodi, Sean O'Callaghan of Tenuta di Carleone and Giampaolo Motta of Tenuta La Massa.

enotecabaldi.it

La Vecchia Nicchia

Via San Martino 12, San Gimignano
+39 0577 573172
enotecalavecchianicchia@gmail.com

Within the walled town of San Gimignano, close to the Porta San Matteo, find La Vecchia Nicchia. Beneath three vaulted arches spans a wine shop and a *bruschetteria* run by husband-and-wife team Alessandro Pieragnoli and Elisa Petrone. Though the shop is within the city walls, it is far from a tourist trap; and it is the fortunate

La Vecchia Nicchia

tourist who finds themselves sitting down to dishes so good they have received their own television show – namely, Ale's inventive gourmet bruschetta, which feature on his regular slot on Gambero Rosso's TV channel. Should you be buying to take away, there are 200 labels to choose from; otherwise, stay put, order a bruschetta and try two of San Gimignano's most invigorating Vernaccia (a varietal white from the region) from Il Colombaio di Santa Chiara and Cappella Sant'Andrea respectively. Or go off-piste and out of the region with Alessandro's top range of extraordinary bubbles – offerings hail from Erpacrife in Piemonte and Podere il Saliceto in Emilia-Romagna.

A Pancia Piena

Piazza Aldo Moro, 9, 50065 Pontassieve FI
+39 370 378 9524

If you are touring and tasting in the Chianti Rufina region, then make your way to Pancia Piena, a food truck specializing in €6 hamburgers (made from organic, zero-kilometre produce) and bottles of exquisite Champagne, like Chavost Blanc d'Assemblage Brut Nature and Egly Ouriet Les Premices. Beyond this novel decadence, there are plates of pasta – from tagliolini with squid ink, calamari and saffron to pici with fresh anchovies, pine nuts and wild fennel blossom – paired with fine wines from Tuscany and Burgundy. These are the wine regions, alongside Champagne, that are loved the most by Emanuele Nenci and Iuri Ronchi, the two friends who opened A Pancia Piena in 2004 with just five bottles of wine by the glass to sell with their panini. All of this, plus techno music (playing at a respectable volume), must account for the euphoric energy from customers – it's all a bit Bacchanalian here. Customers can sign up for A Pancia Piena's wine club to get first dibs on bottles that the pair bring back from their frequent trips to France. If you are staying in the area, do get in touch and see about a mixed case delivery to your holiday home.

instagram.com/apanciapienasieci/

Terra di Piero

Piazza San Francesco, 3, Arezzo

On the first Sunday of every month, the city of Arezzo hosts an enormous antiques fair attracting people from all over the region to the central Piazza Grande. Bargains aplenty are to be found on tables across cobbles sprawling into the surrounding streets, but the real treasures are bottled and on the shelves in adjacent Piazza San

Where winemakers dine

Despite its size, Bolgheri has lots of impressive culinary options, from hearty meat dishes to exquisite seafood. Choosing just one favourite is no easy task, but for me, **Osteria Enoteca San Guido** holds a special place in my heart. This is the kind of restaurant where you immediately feel at home. Every meal promises impeccable service, outstanding ingredients and a menu that never fails to delight. The dishes are a testament to the region's rich culinary heritage, and the quality is unwaveringly top-notch. The wine list is a celebration of Bolgheri's iconic vineyards, with a selection of local masterpieces alongside a few unexpected treasures from other regions. Whether you're a wine enthusiast or simply someone who appreciates good food paired with the perfect glass, Osteria Enoteca San Guido is a true standout in a town already brimming with culinary excellence.

Elena Pozzolini, Tenuta Sette Cieli, Bolgheri

Francesco, inside the Enoteca Terra di Piero. Every week, the wine list by the glass changes, and there are always 18 bottles open to try. The shop has an outstanding range, from the very famous Tuscan names (Masseto) to up-and-coming estates (Bakkanali). You can also seek out wines from Arezzo's top winemakers – Federico Staderini, Filippo Volpi and Stefano Amerighi – to appreciate why this region has a long tradition of fine quality wines. There are even 60 gins to choose from, revealing the owner Cristiano Duranti's passion for spirits and making this enoteca the go-to spot in Arezzo for *aperitivi* and *digestivi*. If you don't manage to do all your wine and spirits shopping in one fell swoop, stock up when you get home: Terra di Piero's online shop is clear and easy to use with the same fabulous selection of wines as in store.

terradipiero.com

Vineria Aperta

Castelnuovo dell'Abate, Montalcino

+39 0577 557083

It's such an enchantingly beautiful drive to Vineria Aperta, heading south as you exit Montalcino and taking the road that passes Biondi-Santi on the left and Abbey Sant'Antimo

Vineria Aperta

on the right, that it might not appear so strange as you begin to approach a beachless beach bar and a sign for 'Landscape Drinking'. This playful wine bar and shop is showcasing and celebrating over 1,500 bottles of terroir-driven wine from across the globe, each one promising to feed both 'thirst and curiosity'. The large list was created and continues to be curated by Sebastian Nasello, the head winemaker of nearby winery Le Ripi, out of a desire to bring together wine lovers and to create a community. (Podere Le Ripi is minutes away for those wishing to add on a visit.) As well as a well-stocked list there are also micro courses and masterclasses on various wine regions, should you find yourself in the area for a few days – plus evenings with DJ sets, 'to combine wine with our passion for electronic music'. The food offering is simple and carefully sourced, designed to support whatever you choose to have poured into your glass. Two flights of wines are available and act as an overview of the region – a selection of four Brunello or six wines to explore the 'Myths and Unicorns' of Montalcino. They each present a very valuable, exquisite afternoon's immersion into the transparency and fluency of Sangiovese and its capacity to sensitively express its origins.

vineriaaperta.com

Ostinati dei Lassi

Ostinati dei Lassi

Via Vecchia Aurelia 54, 57020
La California
+39 3476302022

A five-minute drive north of Bolgheri train station sits the tiny village of La California. And within California lies gold in the form of a wine shop with a food offering that has given reason to rush out of Bolgheri and up the road – particularly the risotto, but also the fine range of cured meats and cheeses. The selection of wines on the shelves and cheeses on the counter is made by owner Massimo Lassi. He has an evident respect for the 'timeless Sassicaia', with an array of vintages on display, but clearly enjoys steering clients towards the smaller, equally premium producers, from I Luoghi to Fabio Motta. Over 1,000 bottles fill the walls, so wine lovers are advised not to plan any estate visits post-lunch, or to perhaps make Ostinati dei Lassi their last stop of the day. This enoteca closes at 10pm for wine sales and food service – and there is no better place in Bolgheri to close the day and begin what will inevitably be a wild night.

instagram.com/_ostinati_deilassi/

Vineria Aperta

Glossary

Annata the vintage year in which the grapes were harvested

Barrique a small oak barrel (usually 225l) often used for ageing wine

Biologica refers to organic viticulture, where chemicals are avoided in the vineyard

Bollicine bubbles, especially in sparkling wines, eg '*una bottiglia di bollicine*'. (qv Frizzante)

Cantina cellar; winery

Cantina Sociale winery cooperative, often shared by small growers

Cascina farmhouse or rural wine estate

Chiaretto a pale wine, slightly lighter than a rosato (qv)

Classico classic; used for the historic heart of a DOC or DOCG region

Colle hill (plural: *colli*)

Collina small hill (plural: *colline*)

Consorzio wine body funded by producers that manages and promotes an appellation

Degustazione tasting, particularly a formal or comparative one

DOC (Denominazione di Origine Controllata) a quality designation that controls production zone, grape varieties and methods

DOCG (Denominazione di Origine Controllata e Garantita) the highest level of Italian wine classification

Ettaro hectare; a unit of area equal to 2.47 acres

Etichetta label, especially a wine label

Fattoria a Tuscan farm, often with wine and olive oil production

Fecce / Feccia sediment or lees from fermentation and ageing

Fiasco the traditional round-bottomed bottle in a straw basket, once typical of Chianti wines

Frizzante a lightly sparkling wine, with gentle bubbles

Gran Selezione the highest category of wine quality for Chianti Classico DOCG

Grappolo (d'uva) a bunch of grapes (plural: *grappoli*)

IGT (Indicazione Geografica Tipica) a more flexible classification that allows experimentation with non-traditional grapes or methods

Lieviti yeast

Metodo Classico sparkling wine method with second fermentation in the bottle

Novello light-bodied wine released shortly after production

Ossidato oxidized, often referring to the negative impact of air

Passito a sweet wine style produced from dried grapes

Pigiatura pressing or crushing of grapes during winemaking

Podere a rural farmstead or vineyard estate, commonly used in Tuscany

Riserva a wine aged longer than standard requirements before release; often higher quality

Rosato a rosé wine

Rosso a red wine, frequently, but not exclusively, used to express a blend

Sangiovese Tuscany's most important red grape variety, forming the basis of many DOC/G wines

Spumante a fully sparkling wine, typically with higher pressure than frizzante (qv)

Superiore a wine with slightly higher alcohol and stricter production standards than regular versions

Super-Tuscan unofficial term for high-quality wines from Tuscany that don't conform to DOC/G rules

Tenuta an estate, often used to describe larger vineyard properties

Terraelectae a special classification for top single-vineyard wines from Chianti Rufina DOCG, introduced to highlight site expression

Terroir the factors that influence a wine's character – soil, climate, topography and human input

Trebbiano a widely-planted white grape used in many Tuscan white wines and Vin Santo

Uvaggio the blend of grape varieties used in a wine

Vendemmia the grape harvest

Vendemmia Tardiva late-harvest wine made from grapes picked after full ripeness, often concentrated and sweet

Vigna vineyard

Vignaiolo winegrower or small-scale winemaker

Vino da Tavola basic table wine category, once used for many Super-Tuscans before IGT was introduced

Vin Santo traditional Tuscan dessert wine made from dried white grapes and aged in small barrels

Vinsantaia the loft or attic where Vin Santo barrels are aged, often exposed to seasonal temperature changes

Zonazione the process of mapping vineyard areas to better understand and manage terroir

Further reading

Fiction/Literature

The Decameron, Giovanni Boccaccio, tr GH McWilliam, Penguin Modern Classics 2003 (written 1349-53)
Ten Florentine nobles escape the plague, and each tells a story a night over 10 days. Some are tragic, some comic and some deliciously bawdy. Written 700 years ago and as relevant as ever.

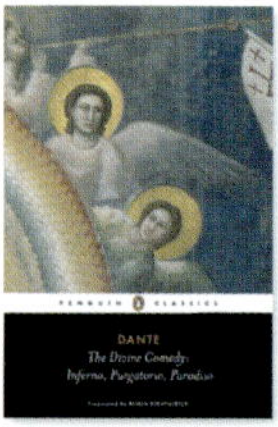

The Divine Comedy, Dante Alighieri, tr Robin Kirkpatrick, Penguin Classics 2012 (written 1308-21)
Begin in the dark wood outside Florence and descend into hell; climb Purgatory, and reach Paradise. You'll never look at a cypress tree the same way again.

A Room with a View, EM Forster, Penguin Classics 2006 (first published 1908)
A young Englishwoman visits Florence and is transformed by its beauty and a scandalous kiss in a field of violets. Forster's most charming work.

The Enchanted April, Elizabeth von Arnim, Virago 1991
Four Englishwomen escape to a Tuscan villa in April and are transformed by sunshine, gardens and silence. Dreamy and timeless.

The Wine-Dark Sea, Leonardo Sciascia (ed. Andrea Camilleri), Granta 2014
Short stories set across Italy, including Tuscany, exploring the intersection of myth, tradition and modern life.

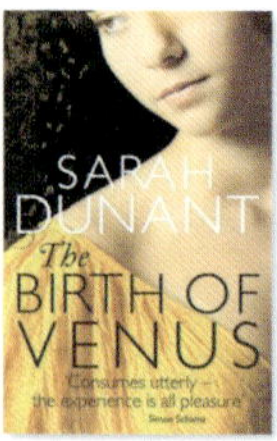

The Birth of Venus, Sarah Dunant, Virago 2013
A historical novel set in 15th-century Florence, about a young woman painter in a time of religious upheaval and Medici intrigue.

The Agony and the Ecstasy, Irving Stone, Arrow 1990 (first published 1961)
A highly readable fictionalized biography of Michelangelo that brings Renaissance Florence and Rome to vivid life.

Dante: Poet of the Secular World, Erich Auerbach, New York Review Books 2007
Analysis of Dante, born and educated in Florence; the Divine Comedy opens in a Tuscan forest.

Biography

Savonarola: The Rise and Fall of a Renaissance Prophet, Donald Weinstein, Yale University Press 2011
Florence's radical preacher, his rise and his execution. Vital for understanding the city's turmoil.

The House of Medici: Its Rise and Fall, Christopher Hibbert, Harper Paperbacks 1999
A richly detailed narrative of the Medici family's power, patronage and occasional poisoning. Essential for understanding Renaissance Florence.

History

Brunelleschi's Dome, Ross King, Vintage 2008
The story of how a goldsmith with no formal architectural training built the dome of Florence Cathedral. A riveting look at Renaissance ingenuity and the fierce politics of the time.

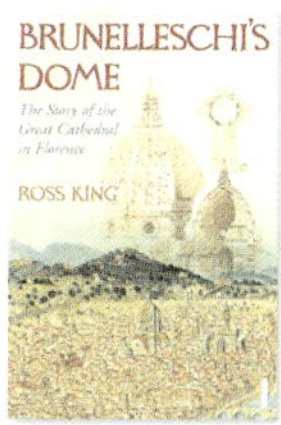

The Stones of Florence, Mary McCarthy, Warbler Classics, 2020
A literary guide to Florence's art, architecture and political past, written with elegance and insight by one of America's veteran critics.

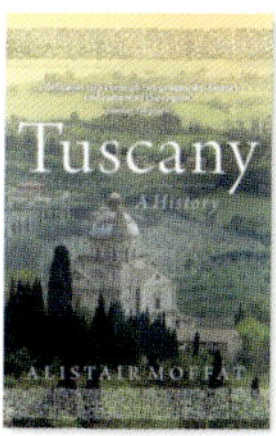

Tuscany: A History, Alistair Moffat, Birlinn 2011
A sweeping account of Tuscany from the Etruscans to the modern era. Rich in anecdote and cultural context.

The Florentines: From Dante to Galileo, Paul Strathern, Atlantic Books 2021
Profiles of the thinkers, artists and patrons who shaped Renaissance Florence.

Dark Water: Art, Disaster, and Redemption in Florence, Robert Clark, Knopf Doubleday 2009
The story of the 1966 flood and how the city rallied to save its art.

The Etruscans, Lucy Shipley, Reaktion Books 2017
An engaging introduction to the ancient people who once ruled much of Tuscany, and whose legacy is still in the soil and stones.

Memoir

Heat, Bill Buford, Vintage 2007
An American journalist heads to Tuscany to work under Dario Cecchini, the world-famous butcher of Panzano. Hilarious, immersive and full of insights into Italian food culture.

A Vineyard in Tuscany: A Wine Lover's Dream, WW Norton 2010
A memoir of buying and restoring a ruined estate in Montalcino, planting vines and making Brunello. Equal parts dream and ordeal.

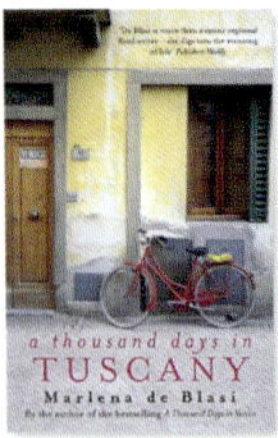

A Thousand Days in Tuscany, Marlena de Blasi, Random House 2005
A food writer moves to a remote Tuscan village. A bestseller.

A Small Place in Italy, Eric Newby, Harper Press 2011 (first published 1994)
Newby – one of the great 20th-century travel writers – recounts his and his wife Wanda's life in a restored farmhouse in the foothills of the Apuan Alps in northern Tuscany (see also Newby's account of being on the run from the Nazis in *Love and War in the Apennines*).

Wine/Food

Chianti Classico: The Search for Tuscany's Noblest Wine, Bill Nesto & Frances Di Savino, University of California Press 2016
Scholarly, readable exploration of Chianti's terroir and identity. Full of wine wisdom.

Under the Tuscan Sun: At Home in Italy, Frances Mayes, Bantam, 2016

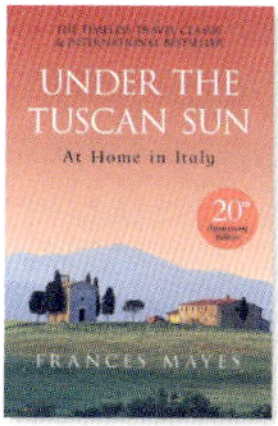

A bestselling memoir about buying and restoring a villa in Cortona. Romantic, and full of recipes and seasonal reflections.

The Tuscan Year, Elizabeth Romer, Macmillan 1985
A month-by-month account of rural Tuscan life, following a farmer's wife through the rhythms of food, family and farming.

Essays/Humour

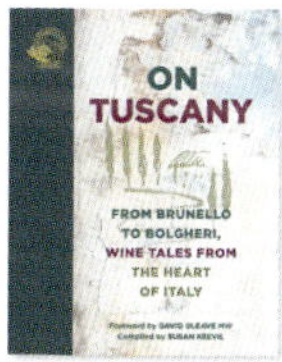

On Tuscany, ed Susan Keevil, Académie du Vin Library 2024
Thirty-eight essays by the world's best wine writers – from Hugh Johnson to Jane Anson – on the food, wine, people and culture of Tuscany. "A love note to the region" (Victoria Moore in the *Telegraph*).

La Bella Figura: A Field Guide to the Italian Mind, Beppe Severgnini, Broadway Books 2006

A witty exploration of the Italian psyche, with plenty of insight into Tuscany's own contradictions.

Index

Acknowledgements

The publishers have made every effort to trace the copyright holders of the text and images reproduced in this book. If, however, you believe that any work has been incorrectly credited or used without permission, please contact us immediately and we will endeavour to rectify the situation.

1 Fattoria Fibbiano, Terricciola, Pisa and Studio Cru, 4br, 90 shutterstock.com/M. Rohana, 5bl, 111 shutterstock.com/StevanZZ, 5br, 167 Bulli&Balene, 4bl, 56 Argentiera Srl, Bolgheri and Studio Cru, 6-7 Le Mortelle, Marchesi Antinori Spa, 8 Giò Martorana, 12-13 shutterstock.com/Kite_rin, 14 J. Paul Getty Museum, 16 Lorenzo Taccioli photographer, 18 shutterstock.com/wjarek, 20 Antinori nel Chianti Classico, Marchesi Antinori Spa, 24 Antonio Cinotti, Marketing and Social Media Manager - Chianti Ultra Trail by UTMB, 26 Consorzio del vino Brunello di Montalcino, 28 Antinori nel Chianti Classico, Marchesi Antinori Spa, 29 Tenuta Argentiera, Argentiera Srl, Bolgheri and Studio Cru, 30 shutterstock.com/iacomino FRiMAGES, 39 Fattoria Fibbiano, Terricciola, Pisa and Studio Cru, 40-41 Società Agricola Tenuta dei Sette Cieli srl and Studio Cru, 42 Azienda Agricola Rascioni & Cecconello, 44 shutterstock.com/Lsdancer, 46 Le Mortelle, Marchesi Antinori Spa, 49 shutterstock.com/Sherri R. Camp, 51 Società Agricola San Felice Spa and Studio Cru, 52 shutterstock.com/ANTONIO TRUZZI, 54 Antinori nel Chianti Classico, Marchesi Antinori Spa, 59 Gert Lucas photographer , 60 Le Mortelle, Marchesi Antinori Spa, 61 Società Agricola San Felice Spa and Studio Cru, 62 Fattoria Fibbiano, Terricciola, Pisa, 64 Tenuta Argentiera, Argentiera Srl, Bolgheri and Studio Cru, 65 Società Agricola San Felice Spa and Studio Cru, 66 Consorzio del vino Brunello di Montalcino, 70, 71 Tenuta Argentiera, Argentiera Srl, Bolgheri and Studio Cru, 72 Fattoria Fibbiano, Terricciola, Pisa and Studio Cru, 76 Cantine Dei, Az. Maria Caterina Dei, 78 Biondi-Santi Archives, 80 Tenuta Argentiera, Argentiera Srl, Bolgheri and Studio Cru, 81 Società Agricola San Felice Spa and Studio Cru, 82 Il Borro Relais & Châteaux, 83 Societa agricola C.I.T.A.I. Spa Tenuta San Guido, 84-85 Biondi-Santi Tenuta Greppo, Le Macchiole Società Agricola s.s., Poderi Boscarelli, Società Agricola Querciabella Spa, COLLEMASSARI S.p.A. Società Agricola, Petrolo Spa, Colombaio Winery, 87 Tenuta Guado al Tasso, Marchesi Antinori Spa, 88-89 Società Agricola San Felice Spa and Studio Cru, 90 shutterstock.com/M. Rohana, 92 shutterstock.com/StevanZZ, 93 MTV Toscana and Cantina Franco Pacenti, Montalcino, 95 Alessandra Molletti and Comune di Greve in Chianti, Firenze, 96 Fabio Guidi photographer and Proloco di Capraia, 97 shutterstock.com/penofoto, 98-99 shutterstock.com/NeverStopLookingUp, 101 shutterstock.com Kuba Puchajda, 102 shutterstock.com/Shadi Alhannat, 105 shutterstock.com/Izabela23, 107 shutterstock.com/SCStock, 109 shutterstock.com/SCStock, 111 shutterstock.com/StevanZZ, 112 shutterstock.com/Rasto SK, 119 shutterstock.com/essevu, 125 shutterstock.com/StevanZZ, 126-127 Tenuta Argentiera, Argentiera Srl, Bolgheri and Studio Cru, 128-129 shutterstock.com/Umomos, 130 Tenuta Argentiera, Argentiera Srl, Bolgheri and Studio Cru, 131 Fattoria Fibbiano, Terricciola, Pisa, 132, 133 Società Agricola Riecine S.r.l, 134 Tenuta Licinia, 135 Tenuta Sette Ponti , 136, 137 Tenuta Argentiera, Argentiera Srl, Bolgheri, 138TL Società Agricola Ampeleia srl, 138br Castello di Vicarello, Grosseto, 139 Società Agricola San Felice Spa, 141tl Tenute Ruffino s.r.l. società agricola, 141br Castello di Meleto, Siena, 142 La Casaccia di Franceschi s.s. Società Agricola, 143 Il Borro Relais & Châteaux, 145 Capanna Suites, agriturismo, spa and wine club, 146 Tenuta Sette Ponti, 147 Rosewood Castiglion del Bosco, Montalcino, 148 Ristorante Rinuccio 1180, Marchesi Antinori Spa, 150 Cantine Dei, Az. Maria Caterina Dei, 152 Ristorante Rinuccio 1180, Marchesi Antinori Spa, 153 Società Agricola Usiglian del Vescovo S.r.l., 154 Osteria di Passignano, Marchesi Antinori Spa, 156 Osteria Enoteca San Guido, Societa' agricola C.I.T.A.I. Spa Tenuta San Guido, 157 Famiglia Cecchi, 158 Osteria del Tasso, Tenuta Guado al Tasso, Marchesi Antinori Spa, 159 Santa Elisabetta fine dining restaurant at Hotel Brunelleschi, Firenze, 160 Fattoria Fibbiano, Terricciola, Pisa, 161tl Atto di Vito Mollica, 161br Angel Drink & Dine at Calimala Hotel, Firenze, 163tl Le Logge del Vignola, 163br Societa agricola Bulichella s.r.l., 164 Osteria del Tasso, Tenuta Guado al Tasso, Marchesi Antinori Spa, 165 Lux Lucis at Principe Forte dei Marmi hotel, 166 Lux Lucis at Principe Forte dei Marmi hotel, 169 Gilli 1733 s.r.l., 170 Tua Rita, Suvereto, 171tl Cibrèo Caffè at Helvetia & Bristol Hotel Firenze, 172 Il Santino, Enoteca e gastronomia, Firenze, 173tl Locale, Firenze, 173br Tenuta Licinia, 174-175 Bulli&Balene, 176 Antica Macelleria Cecchini, Panzano in Chianti, Firenze, 178 Osteria Vini e Vecchi Sapori, Firenze, 179 Trattoria Cibrèo, Firenze, 181 Antica Macelleria Cecchini, Panzano in Chianti, Firenze, 182 la Bottega di Elena, Bolgheri, 183 Arduino Bolgheri Osteria Ancestrale, Castagneto Carducci, Livorno, 184 Teatro del Mare, Piombino, 185 Trattoria Cammillo, Firenze, 186 La Vecchia Nicchia di Alessandro Pieragnoli Enoteca - Bruschetteria, San Gimignano, 188 Formaggioteca Terroir, Firenze, 189tl Enoteca Baldi, Panzano in Chianti, Firenze, 189br Poggio Antico, Montalcino , 190 La Vecchia Nicchia di Alessandro Pieragnoli Enoteca - Bruschetteria, San Gimignano, 192 Società Agricola Tenuta dei Sette Cieli srl and Studio Cru, 193 Vineria Aperta Montalcino , 194 OstiNati dei Lassi Enoteca con Cucina, Livorno, 195 Vineria Aperta Montalcino

Also available in

The Smart Traveller's Wine Guide series

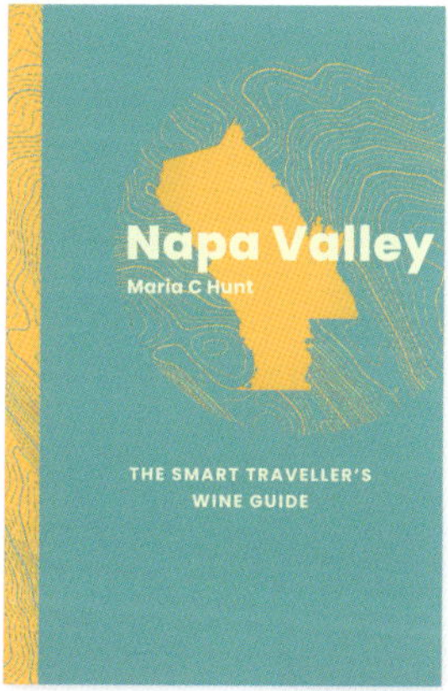

COMING SOON:

Rhône Valley | Switzerland

ACADEMIE DU VIN LIBRARY

www.academieduvinlibrary.com

Other books from Académie du Vin Library we think you'll enjoy

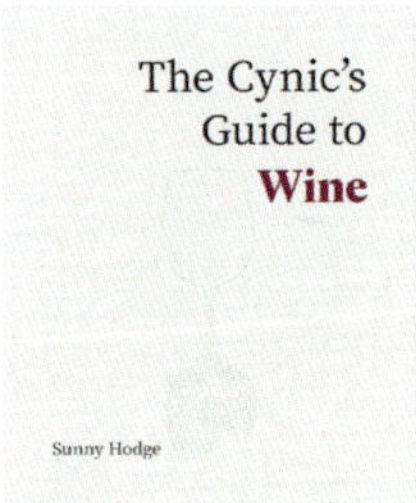

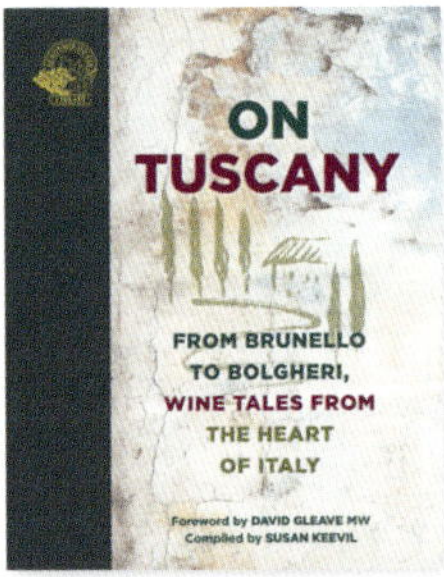

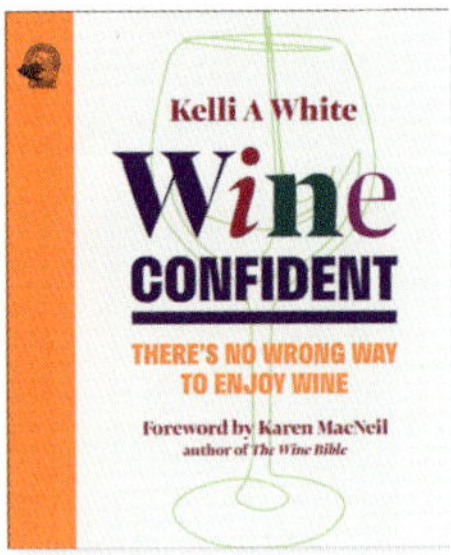

www.academieduvinlibrary.com